Towards Pedestrian-Friendly Neighbourhoods

Promoting walk culture in the Indian cities

Dedicated to
all the walk lovers

Towards Pedestrian-Friendly Neighbourhoods
Promoting walk culture in the Indian cities

Meenakshi Singhal

COPAL PUBLISHING GROUP
Inspiring for a better future through publishing

Published by Copal Publishing Group
E-143, Lajpat Nagar, Sahibabad,
Distt. Ghaziabad, UP – 201005, India

www.copalpublishing.com

First Published 2019
© Copal Publishing Group, 2019

This book contains information obtained from authentic and highly regarded sources. Reprinted material is quoted with permission. Reasonable efforts have been made to publish reliable data and information, but the authors and the publishers cannot assume responsibility for the validity of all materials. Neither the authors nor the publishers, nor anyone else associated with this publication, shall be liable for any loss, damage or liability directly or indirectly caused or alleged to be caused by this book.

Neither this book nor any part may be reproduced or transmitted in any form or by any means, electronic or mechanical, including photocopying, microfilming and recording, or by any information storage or retrieval system, without permission in writing from Copal Publishing Group. The consent of Copal Publishing Group does not extend to copying for general distribution, for promotion, for creating new works, or for resale. Specific permission must be obtained in writing from Copal Publishing Group for such copying.

The Author hereby warrants that the Work is original work, that it does not infringe any other copyright. The Publisher is not in anyway responsible for any legal proceedings and expense whatsoever in consequence of the publication or alleged publication in the Work of any pirated, libellous, seditious, scandalous, obscene or other unlawful matter.

Trademark notice: Product or corporate names may be trademarks or registered trademarks, and are used only for identification and explanation, without intent to infringe.

ISBN: 978-93-83419-79-1 (Print)
ISBN: 978-93-83419-80-7 (e-book)

Typeset by Bhumi Graphics, New Delhi
Printed and bound by Bhavish Graphics, Chennai

Contents

Contents	*v*
Preface	*vii*
Foreword	*ix*
About the Author	*xi*
List of Abbreviations	*xii*
List of Tables	*xiv*
List of Figures	*xv*
Introduction	*xix*

1. Vanishing Pedestrian in the Urban Scene — 1
   1.1 Pedestrian and Walk Behaviour — 1
   1.2 Walk-Friendly Traditional City Cores — 2
   1.3 Vehicle Invasion and the Pedestrian Narrative — 3
   1.4 Current Pedestrian Scenario in the Indian Cities — 6
   1.5 Discourses on Walking: Merely a Fad or a Worldwide Necessity — 9
   1.6 Visibility of Pedestrian in the Emerging Urban Planning and Design Movements — 10
   1.7 Conclusion — 14

2. In Quest for the Pedestrian Revival — 16
   2.1 What Determines the Walk Behaviour? — 16
   2.2 Neighbourhood as an Urban Planning Module — 18
   2.3 Appropriateness of Neighbourhoods for Promoting Pedestrian Culture — 20
   2.4 Impact of the Built Environment on Pedestrian Mobility — 21
   2.5 Global Policies for Promoting Walk Culture — 31
   2.6 Global Practices for Enhanced Walkability — 36
   2.7 Conclusion — 39

3. **Pedestrian Awakening in the Indian Cities** 42
   3.1 Exploring Pedestrian Concerns in the Existing Policy Framework and Legislation 42
   3.2 Initiatives at Enhancing Walkability in Indian Cities 56
   3.3 Conclusion 59

4. **Walk Scenario in the Neighbourhoods of Amritsar City: A Case Study** 65
   4.1 Amritsar City: An Overview of Traffic and Pedestrian Scenario 65
   4.2 Selecting Neighbourhoods of Amritsar City for Further Investigation 69
   4.3 Developing Framework for the Assessment of Neighbourhood Walkability 72
   4.4 Observations Regarding Responsiveness of Neighbourhood Built Environment to the Pedestrian Concerns 89
   4.5 Observations Regarding Residents' Attitudes and Perceptions 118
   4.6 Findings for walk scenario in the neighbourhoods of Amritsar city 127

5. **The Way Forward** 131
   5.1 Application of Pedestrian-Friendly Principles in the Neighbourhoods of Amritsar City 131
   5.2 Recommendations for Pedestrian-Friendly Neighbourhood Environment in the Indian Cities 137

Bibliography 140
Annexure I: Pedestrian Environmental Data Scan (PEDS) Audit Tool 146
Annexure II: Parameters and Attributes of Walkability Survey 147
Annexure III: Proforma for Field Walkability Survey at Segment Level 152
Annexure IV: Questionnaire for Pedestrian Perception and Preference Survey 154
Annexure V: Scores and Weights Assigned to the Parameters and Attributes of Walkability Survey 155

Index 161

Preface

Walking has always remained the most intrinsic and most prevalent of all human mobility means. Despite the fact that the current urbanization and mobility trends have badly bruised the pedestrian realm, the benefits of walking can't be denied or undermined even with the utmost level of development. The present day cities seem to have lost the pedestrian culture in the maze of rapidly escalating vehicular traffic, but the voices calling for reinventing walking are also getting vociferous. Having realized the impact that built environment can make in enhancing or obliterating the pedestrian culture, the professionals across the world are trying to modulate their built environments from pedestrian perspective. Various policies and strategies are formulated, guidelines are prepared and specific proposals are implemented across the globe; and the Indian cities too have started responding to these changing attitudes. In India, awareness becomes visible in the form of relevant policies, norms and partial attempts, but this move needs to gather momentum. Walkability is mainly getting addressed either in terms of developing pedestrian infrastructure along major arterials in the cities or pedestrianizing certain important streets of the cities. The prototypes at neighbourhood level that may serve as an inspiration are grossly lacking. However, templates are developed for various street widths that may serve as a forerunner in this direction.

The present book is an attempt towards furthering and reinforcing the pedestrian spirits at neighbourhood level. Promoting and reinforcing pedestrian culture at the neighbourhood or area level shall be highly instrumental in injecting walking spirits into the daily lives of the residents. Further, this targets everybody equally irrespective of socio-economic and cultural variations. The widely acknowledged principles related to 'pedestrian-friendly neighbourhoods' are investigated in the diverse neighbourhoods of Amritsar city that may eventually form an assertion for effectuating pedestrian-related improvement initiatives in the city. The city offers enough diversity in its neighbourhoods and serves as an envoy of several other metropolitan cities in the country. Therefore, lessons learnt may be largely or wholly implementable in many metropolitan cities in India.

This book entitled *"Towards Pedestrian-Friendly Neighbourhoods: Promoting Walk Culture in the Indian Cities"* is inspired, extracted and adapted from my PhD thesis entitled *"Pedestrian Oriented Planning and Design of Neighbourhoods: Measuring and Evaluating the Walkability of Diverse Neighbourhoods in Amritsar City"* submitted to Guru Nanak Dev University (GNDU), Amritsar.

In this endeavour of mine, I wish to place a debt of gratitude to my mentor and distinguished supervisor Prof. (Dr.) Karamjit Singh Chahal of the Department of Architecture, Guru Nanak Dev University (GNDU), Amritsar for his valuable guidance and willing cooperation during the course of my PhD thesis. I am extremely indebted to GNDU Authorities for facilitating me and extending cooperation in the successful accomplishment of this task. I warmly thank Amritsar Development Authority and Amritsar Improvement Trust for reinforcing me with essential information; and also the faculty members of the Department of Architecture and GRD School of Planning, GNDU, Amritsar for extensive discussions around my work and suggestions that helped refine my research work. I have special gratitude for Prof. (Dr.) Parminder Singh, Department of Economics, GNDU, Amritsar, whose extensive knowledge and research experience was highly beneficial. I am equally thankful to the students of Department of Architecture who sat through intensive interactive sessions and conducted the requisite surveys.

Last but not the least, I would like to thank my husband Vikas Nohria and my sons Siddharth Nohria and Nipun Nohria for their unstinted support and encouragement that made it possible for me to accomplish this task successfully. Above all, I thank the Almighty for all the blessings showered on me during the course of this endeavour.

Dr. Meenakshi Singhal
Department of Architecture
Guru Nanak Dev University, Amritsar

Foreword

Walking is an essential condition for fostering soft mobility. It has become a topical issue of urban sustainability policies in several countries. In their various phases of economic development, many countries have witnessed an uncontrolled growth in the rate of private motorization at the cost of compromising upon the livability and proper functioning of cities and towns. The deleterious effects of mass motorization are fast becoming an urban reality in India as well.

Reinventing walking as an alternative to the avoidable use of private car is a significant step forward in case of developing countries like India, whereby the amount of trips on foot or bicycle still represents a high share of daily displacements in the urban areas – a scenario that needs to be preserved and enhanced with appropriate policies and design.

In that sense, the book is focused on a very relevant concern of the contemporary city. The book has the merit of addressing the theme which is important for the sustainable development of Indian cities, taking advantage of the experiences and studies carried out in the urban contexts of other countries.

The physical environment that surrounds us plays an enormous role in defining and modulating our behaviors, and thereby our mobility patterns. While interrogating the built environments that have triggered unsustainable mobility practices is absolutely opportune; neighbourhoods, as absolutely feasible modules to promote walking, have additional potential to impact upon the residents of all income categories equally.

The book, through the walkability assessment of wide-ranging neighbourhoods of an Indian city, offers a knowledge base to pedestrian-related improvement initiatives in the city as also a methodology which may be applied in other urban contexts in India.

The book is well structured and clearly written. It brings forth the urgency of improving Amritsar city's neighbourhood walking environment, providing scientific background for intervention at the same time offering specific recommendations based on systematic and tailored on characteristics and needs of each part of the city.

It propagates for replication of similar studies in the other urban areas of the country, where mass motorization is increasing along with the neglect and decay of urban pedestrian infrastructure. The book shall be immensely useful in policy making and making priority decisions with regard to what improvement actions may be taken.

Prof. (Dr.) Mandeep Singh
(B.Arch., Master of Urban Design, PhD)
Head Architecture & Former Dean
Former Head Urban Design & Former Head Industrial Design
School of Planning and Architecture, New Delhi

About the Author

Dr. Meenakshi Singhal is an Associate Professor in the Department of Architecture (Faculty of Physical Planning and Architecture) at Guru Nanak Dev University (GNDU), Amritsar. She has more than twenty five years of teaching experience. She graduated from Chandigarh College of Architecture (CCA), Chandigarh, and obtained M.Tech. in Urban Planning from GNDU, Amritsar. She attained All India Rank (AIR)-4 in GATE-2013 (Architecture and Planning), and received Silver Medal in her Post-Graduate studies. In 2018, she was awarded the Degree of Doctor of Philosophy in Architecture by GNDU, Amritsar based on her research work entitled "Pedestrian Oriented Planning and Design of Neighbourhoods: Measuring and Evaluating the Walkability of Diverse Neighbourhoods in Amritsar City".

Her research interests relate to 'Sustainability Concerns in Architecture and Planning' and 'Quality of Urban Spaces'. She has almost 24 publications in the Refereed Indian Journals and in the Proceedings of International and National Conferences/Seminars. She represented her institution in the 6th Annual International Conference on "Architecture and Civil Engineering (ACE-2018)" organized by Global Science and Technology Forum (GSTF) from 14-15 May 2018 in Singapore as Paper Presenter.

At the institution level, she has been entrusted with various administrative responsibilities. She performed additional responsibility as the Warden of the Girls Hostel (2012–2015) and as the Head of Architecture Department (2015-2018). She was a member of Planning Board (2015-2017) and Academic Council (2015-18) of the University.

Dr. Meenakshi Singhal
B.Arch., M.Tech. (Urban Planning), Ph.D. (Architecture)
Associate Professor and Former Head, Department of Architecture
Guru Nanak Dev University, Amritsar, Punjab State, India
Email: meenakshi_gndu@yahoo.com; meenakshi.arch@gndu.ac.in

List of Abbreviations

ANOVA	:	Analysis of Variance
BRT	:	Bus Rapid Transport
CAI-Asia	:	Clean Air Initiative for Asian Cities
CDP	:	City Development Plan
CNU	:	Congress for the New Urbanism
CPCB	:	Central Pollution Control Board
CSE	:	Centre for Science and Environment
CUBEST	:	China Urban Built Environment Scan Tool
DDA	:	Delhi Development Authority
EPC	:	Environmental Planning Collaborative
GIS	:	Geographic Information System
HOV lanes	:	High Occupancy Vehicle lanes
IPC	:	Indian Penal Code
IRC	:	Indian Roads Congress
ITDP	:	Institute for Transportation and Development Policy
IUT	:	Institute of Urban Transport
JNNURM	:	Jawaharlal Nehru Urban Renewable Mission
LOS	:	Level of Service
MoRTH	:	Ministry of Road Transport and Highways
MRT	:	Mass Rapid Transport
NEWS	:	Neighbourhood Environment Walkability Scale

NMT	:	Non-Motorized Transport
NMV	:	Non-Motorized Vehicle
NTDPC	:	National Transport Development Policy Committee
NUTP	:	National Urban Transport Policy
NURM	:	National Urban Renewal Mission
MoUD	:	Ministry of Urban Development
PEDS	:	Pedestrian Environment Data Scan
PERS	:	Pedestrian Environment Review System
pph	:	Persons Per Hectare
PT	:	Public Transport
ROW	:	Right-Of-Way
SPSS	:	Statistical Package for the Social Sciences
TOD	:	Transit-Oriented Development
TND	:	Traditional Neighbourhood Development
TRIPP	:	Transport Research and Injury Prevention Programme
UTTIPEC	:	Unified Traffic and Transportation Infrastructure, Planning and Engineering Centre
WHO	:	World Health Organization

List of Tables

Table no.	Title	Page no.
Table 1.1	Population-based walkability data for selected Indian cities	8
Table 2.1	Variables and indicators of built environment determining pedestrian mobility	22
Table 3.1	Level of Service (LOS) criteria for width of sidewalk	49
Table 4.1	Modal share in Amritsar	67
Table 4.2	Neighbourhoods of Amritsar city selected for investigation	72
Table 4.3	Overview of selected pedestrian audit tools	75
Table 4.4	Selected parameters and attributes of study	77
Table 4.5	Number and length of segments surveyed in the selected neighbourhoods	78
Table 4.6	Subjective assessment of street segments in selected neighbourhoods	93
Table 4.7	Overall walkability scores based on segment-level parameters	100
Table 4.8	ANOVA based on neighbourhoods	115
Table 4.9	ANOVA based on population density	116
Table 4.10	Socio-economic profile of the respondents	118
Table 4.11	Walk perception and preferences of the respondents	119
Table 4.12	Chi-square tests to measure association	120
Table 4.13	Crosstab Test to measure the Degree of Association with population density	121
Table 4.14	Crosstab Test to measure the Degree of Association with monthly household income	122
Table 4.15	List of desired improvements in the pedestrian environment	123
Table 4.16	Residents' rankings and weighted averages for desired improvements	124
Table 4.17	Weighted averages for desired improvements based on population density	125
Table 4.18	Weighted averages for desired improvements based on monthly household income	126

List of Figures

Figure no.	Title	Page no.
Figure 1.1	Traditional city cores: Walled City, Amritsar, and Shahjahanabad, Delhi	3
Figure 1.2	Registered vehicles per 1000 population in India	4
Figure 1.3	Modal split of registered vehicles (percent) for the year 2012	4
Figure 1.4	Example of Traditional Neighbourhood Development	13
Figure 2.1	Variables impacting on pedestrian mobility	17
Figure 2.2	Clarence A. Perry's Neighbourhood Unit of 1929	19
Figure 2.3	Desirable modal preference in a metropolitan city	20
Figure 2.4	Average walking distance	21
Figure 2.5	Image depicting distinction between connectivity and permeability	23
Figure 2.6	Diagrammatic depiction of transportation network in Vauban, Freiburg, Germany	24
Figure 2.7	Impact of street networks on pedestrians	25
Figure 2.8	Impact of street facades on pedestrians	26
Figure 2.9	Visual enclosure for spatial definition	27
Figure 2.10	Impact of right trees at the right location	28
Figure 2.11	Impact of street corners on crossing distance	29
Figure 2.12	Placement of pedestrian amenities ideally in the fixture/planting zone	30
Figure 2.13	Traffic-calming devices	37
Figure 3.1	Three distinct footpath zones	48
Figure 3.2	Kerb height	50
Figure 3.3	Location of kerb ramps at street intersection	50
Figure 3.4	Views of kerb ramp cut into the pavement	51

Figure 3.5	Guide blocks and warning blocks forming guiding path to the building	51
Figure 3.6	Multifunctional zone on a street	53
Figure 3.7	Lighting on the footpath	54
Figure 3.8	At-grade pedestrian crossings	55
Figure 3.9	Typical pedestrian refuge at median	56
Figure 3.10	Templates for 24 m and 18 m roads with mixed-use zones	57
Figure 3.11	Templates for 6 m wide streets (with shared spaces)	60
Figure 3.12	Templates for 7.5 m wide streets	61
Figure 3.13	Templates for 9 m wide streets	62
Figure 4.1	Share of walk trips (percent) for the selected cities	67
Figure 4.2	Walkability Index for the selected cities	68
Figure 4.3	Spatial distribution of the selected neighbourhoods in Amritsar city	71
Figure 4.4	Glimpses of 'general street environment' in the neighbourhoods of Amritsar city	83
Figure 4.5	Glimpses of 'pathway availability and quality' in the neighbourhoods of Amritsar city	84
Figure 4.6	Glimpses of 'obstructions to walking' in the neighbourhoods of Amritsar city	85
Figure 4.7	Glimpses of 'traffic safety' in the neighbourhoods of Amritsar city	86
Figure 4.8	Glimpses of 'pedestrian amenities' in the neighbourhoods of Amritsar city	87
Figure 4.9	Glimpses of 'spatial quality' in the neighbourhoods of Amritsar city	88
Figure 4.10	Prevalence (percent) of various types of buildings/land uses	89
Figure 4.11	Prevalence (percent) of various types of pedestrian paths	90
Figure 4.12	Prevalence (percent) of various kerb types	90
Figure 4.13	Prevalence (percent) of various permanent and temporary obstructions	90

Figure 4.14	Prevalence (percent) of various crossing aids and traffic-calming devices	91
Figure 4.15	Prevalence (percent) of various pedestrian amenities	92
Figure 4.16	Prevalence (percent) of street orientation of buildings	93
Figure 4.17	Prevalence (percent) of natural sights	93
Figure 4.18	Subjective assessment (percent) of street segments in the selected neighbourhoods	94
Figure 4.19	Objectively assessed walkability scores for general street environment	98
Figure 4.20	Objectively assessed walkability scores for pathway availability and quality	98
Figure 4.21	Objectively assessed walkability scores for obstructions to walking	98
Figure 4.22	Objectively assessed walkability scores for traffic safety	99
Figure 4.23	Objectively assessed walkability scores for pedestrian amenities	99
Figure 4.24	Objectively assessed walkability scores for spatial quality	99
Figure 4.25	Walkability scores based on subjective assessment	99
Figure 4.26	Overall walkability scores based on segment level parameters	**100**
Figure 4.27	Street sections and pedestrian scenario in Katra Karam Singh (N-1)	101
Figure 4.28	Street sections and pedestrian scenario in Bagh Ramanand (N-2)	102
Figure 4.29	Street sections and pedestrian scenario in Kashmir Avenue (N-3)	103
Figure 4.30	Street sections and pedestrian scenario in Dayanand Nagar (N-4)	104
Figure 4.31	Street sections and pedestrian scenario in Basant Avenue (N-5)	105
Figure 4.32	Street sections and pedestrian scenario in Rani ka Bagh (N-6)	106

Figure 4.33	Street sections and pedestrian scenario in Green Avenue (N-7)	107
Figure 4.34	Street sections and pedestrian scenario in B-Block, Ranjit Avenue (N-8)	108
Figure 4.35	Street sections and pedestrian scenario in Defence Colony (N-9)	109
Figure 4.36	Street sections and pedestrian scenario in Housing Board Colony (N-10)	110
Figure 4.37	Street sections and pedestrian scenario in Mohan Nagar (N-11)	111
Figure 4.38	Street sections and pedestrian scenario in New Amritsar (N-12)	112
Figure 4.39	Street sections and pedestrian scenario in Bhalla Colony (N-13)	113
Figure 4.40	Street sections and pedestrian scenario in Holy City (N-14)	114
Figure 4.41	Desired improvements based on population density	126
Figure 4.42	Desired improvements based on monthly household income	127
Figure 5.1	Proposed layout for 7.5 m and 9 m wide streets in Amritsar city	134
Figure 5.2	Proposed layout for 12 m and 15 m wide streets in Amritsar city	135
Figure 5.3	Proposed layout for 18 m and 20 m wide streets in Amritsar city	136
Figure 5.4	Proposed layout at the road intersections	137

Introduction

"Automobiles are often conveniently tagged as the villains responsible for the ills of cities and the disappointments and futilities of city planning. But the destructive effects of automobiles are much less a cause than a symptom of our incompetence at city building."
(Jacobs, 1992)

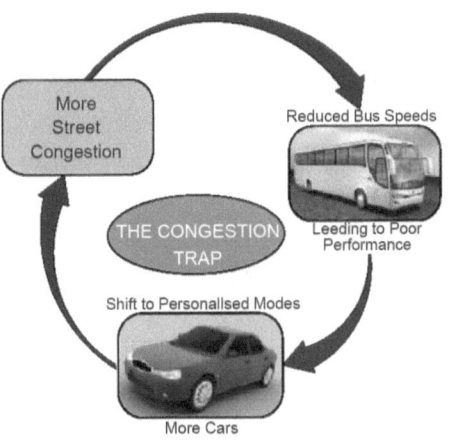

Cities are considered the engines of economic growth. In the hard endeavor to achieve economic prosperity of our cities, rapid urbanization got triggered and transport demand became an obvious appendage. The general response of city planning has invariably been provision of an effective transport network which rather eased out more vehicles on the roads thus creating a vicious circle of expanding road capacities to more vehicles to traffic congestions. The ensuing reduced speed of public transport caused the societies to shift to personalized modes which, being low on carrying capacity but high on road occupancy, have turned out to be the greatest menace. The consequences are for all the societies to see and bear. The ever-rising vehicle invasion into the city structure is having severe repercussions on our health, environment, social cohesiveness and economic growth. Consensus in the international circles is emerging that expanding transport network may just be an interim approach; rather the transport demand and supply should be managed in a holistic manner to attain sustainable transport solutions.

"The simple needs of automobiles are more easily understood and satisfied than the complex needs of cities, and a growing number of planners and designers have come to believe that if they can only solve the problems of traffic, they will thereby have solved the major problem of cities. Cities have much more intricate economic and social concerns than automobile traffic. How can you know what to try with traffic until you know how the city itself works, and what else it needs to do with its streets?
You can't." (Jacobs, 1992)

Walking is an integral part of the whole transport system. However, conventional land use and transport planning practices in Indian cities still pay little attention to walking. Walking has always remained the most elementary of all human mobility means. It is the most prevalent human activity that transcends all categories of social, cultural, economic, geographical and temporal divisions or boundaries. With the fast pace of urbanization and the consequent mobility explosion, this basic human instinct got a huge setback as the towns and cities gradually succumbed to the whims and fancies of the motorists. However, various health, environmental and socio-cultural concerns in the contemporary times are prompting societies across the globe to revive walk cultures in their respective jurisdictions by modulating their built environments. Pedestrian mobility triggers social relationships and instills mutual confidence amongst the people that battles social unrest and crimes. It causes intimacy with the physical environment around causing enhanced sense of security and safety. As stated by Allan B. Jacobs in the "Great Streets",

"You don't meet other people while driving in a private car, nor often in a bus or trolley. It's on foot that you see people's faces and statures and that you meet and experience them. That is how public socializing and community enjoyment in daily life can most easily occur. And it's on foot that one can be most intimately involved with the urban environment; with stores, houses, the natural environment, and with people"
(SANDAG, 2002).

In this regard, the book entitled **"Towards Pedestrian-Friendly Neighbourhoods: Promoting Walk Culture in the Indian Cities"** is a modest attempt towards promoting walk culture at neighbourhood area level in the Indian cities. The book is divided into five chapters –

Chapter 1: Vanishing Pedestrian in the Urban Scene
Chapter 2: In Quest for the Pedestrian Revival
Chapter 3: Pedestrian Awakening in the Indian Cities

Chapter 4: Walk Scenario in the Neighbourhoods of Amritsar City: A Case Study

Chapter 5: The Way Forward

Chapter 1 first spells out the meaning of a pedestrian and his walk behaviour. While our traditional cities stand glorified for their humane and pedestrian spirits, the contemporary cities have turned out to be nightmarish experience for the pedestrians. In this light, the pedestrian apathy in the era of high mobility is brought forth, supported by factual data, specifically in the context of Indian cities. While the various dialogues on sustainable development reflect walking as an inevitable ingredient; various recent planning movements too attempt to address the pedestrian concerns in a larger way. It, therefore, emerges that our urban areas must offer themselves as livable places for the benefit of the pedestrians.

Chapter 2 sets forth to explore the forces that determine the pedestrian behaviour. Most suitable module for promoting walk ethos is being explored. For the planners, architects and similar professionals, the built environment is the prime concern which therefore is explored more intensively. Most efforts for promoting pedestrian infrastructure focus along major arterials in the cities or along selected important streets of the cities. However, the study believes that a neighbourhood would be the most relevant city module since it signifies the instilling of walk culture into the daily lives of all categories of city residents. Policies and practices in the other cities across the globe are discussed that create a strong support in this endeavor.

Chapter 3 explores the relevant policies and legislations in the Indian context that may support the pedestrian initiative in the neighbourhoods of Amritsar city. Though the Indian urban development and transportation policies too have gradually started reflecting the pedestrian concerns, our cities still remain in the nascent stage of developing and adopting pedestrian-oriented practices. Certain isolated attempts are there but this movement needs to gather momentum. Actual implementation must see the light of the day so that the experiences generated may be further replicated or evolved for the better. The stakeholders of development too need to be identified, suitably empowered and made accountable. In the process, it becomes pertinent to explore how our Indian cities, in terms of their built environments, respond to the pedestrians' imminent needs and inherent desires. Case studies in this regard may be a step forward.

Chapter 4 investigates the built environments of the neighbourhoods of Amritsar city. The selection of Amritsar city for the purpose was based on the fact that the various phases of physical growth and development of the city since its inception in the 16th century have generated variety in its neighbourhoods; thus it could serve as a potential representative of several metropolitan cities of India. A framework is prepared based on researches conducted in various countries. The Pedestrian Environmental Data Scan (PEDS), the environmental audit tool developed and tested in United States, was adapted to create the *Audit Performa*. The two-page *Audit Performa* so developed and contextualized is comprehensive and values both objective and subjective assessments. *Scoring criteria* for various parameters and attributes was established based on the literature reviewed. In essence seven parameters *(General Street Environment, Pathway Availability & Quality, Obstructions to Walking, Traffic Safety, Disability Infrastructure, Pedestrian Amenities and Spatial Quality)* comprising 34 attributes are figured out for further enquiry. A total of 14 neighbourhoods are judiciously identified from varied density zones of Amritsar city for the purpose of rigorous investigation. The chapter also develops the framework for seeking the residents' feedback for ensuring wider social acceptability of implementation efforts.

A nationwide assessment of 30 selected cities in 2008 by the Union Ministry of Urban Development, Government of India, for the purpose of formulating traffic- and transportation-related policies and strategies in the urban areas of India indicates that though the share of walk trips in Amritsar city is higher than the national average, walkability conditions are much more formidable. Expecting an equally dismal a scenario in its neighbourhoods, it is being hypothized that the built environments of the varied neighbourhoods in Amritsar do not appropriately respond to the pedestrian context. Therefore, this chapter seeks to investigate the built environments of varied neighbourhoods of Amritsar city from pedestrian perspective utilizing relevant variables and attributes; and to determine the residents' attitudes and preferences towards walking. The study is based on the premise that the physical attributes of neighbourhoods can influence walking behaviors, and that the residents' feedback would largely determine the success or failure of any relevant improvement initiatives. The chapter concludes in terms of findings for the neighbourhood walkability scenario in Amritsar city. It emerges from the empirical analysis that the neighbourhood streets of Amritsar are deficient in most walkability-related features. However, the spatial quality is somewhat favorable. In general, it may be understood that the neighbourhoods have a huge potential for improvement.

There were a number of confounds and problems with this study. To begin with, data availability was a big issue. While the classification of the various neighbourhoods into broad population density zones was derived from the Draft Master Plan (2010-31) document, the density implications of individual neighbourhoods got overshadowed within those broad zones. The neighbourhoods themselves were delineated based on Google Maps. Then there were issues in logically weighing the relative importance of each parameter. Walkability research in the past has based itself on myriad features without being conclusive of their relative importance. This created problems in allocating weightages to the varied parameters. Further, the complications in discreetly identifying the impact of individual attributes on pedestrians were many, and their huge number and complex nature tended to baffle the perception of the Audit teams.

Chapter 5, based on the empirical findings, recommends the immediate upgradation of 14 selected neighbourhoods for the pedestrian benefit to serve as a prototype to propagate the spirit of walking in the other neighbourhoods of Amritsar city as also several other cities in the country. Suitable templates are developed for this purpose that may serve as ready-reckoners. The other cities should also derive inspiration and follow the suit.

Walkability research has to a large extent remained theoretical only. It is time to move towards implementation so that real-time benefits derived out of the enhanced neighbourhood environment may be studied, quantified and compared. However, implementation in the existing neighbourhoods may not be easy because of the limitations of street width, general non-willingness of car users to transform themselves for the sake of pedestrian environment and several other factors. In this context, meticulous planning followed by strict implementation would have to be ensured by the concerned agencies especially in the current socio-cultural scenario.

1
Vanishing Pedestrian in the Urban Scene

Walking has always remained the most elementary of all human mobility means. It is the most prevalent human activity that transcends all categories of social, cultural, economic, geographical and temporal divisions or boundaries. However, with the fast pace of urbanization and the consequent mobility explosion, this basic human instinct got a huge setback as the towns and cities gradually succumbed to the whims and fancies of the motorists. The large scale intrusion of vehicles impacted on the city fabric, modulating its scale, treatment and expanse while ghastly eroding its pedestrian culture. As the negative environmental, social and health implications of this new trend are surfacing and getting realized, efforts galore are made across the globe to revive the pedestrian culture in the garb of sustainability agenda.

In this context, this chapter highlights the pedestrian sensitivity of the traditional city structure in contrast to the much bruised pedestrian realm of the contemporary motorized societies. Deep concerns are raised regarding the vanishing of the pedestrian from the urban realm, reasons are explored thereof and the virtues of walking are reinvented and realized. The unfailing appearance of the pedestrian in the prevalent planning movements or philosophies signifies the resolve of the modern societies to bring walking back into the mainstream of urban living.

1.1 Pedestrian and Walk Behaviour

Simply speaking, any person on foot is a pedestrian. The term, however, encompasses a huge diversity of road users that vary widely in their physical and cognitive abilities. While the general perception is that of an able-bodied pedestrian, it also includes all those who are in a wheelchair or on a skateboard or pushing a pram, etc. New Zealand Pedestrian Planning and Design Guide (2008) defines pedestrian as "a person on foot, or in or on a contrivance equipped with wheels or revolving runners that is not a vehicle". As per Indian Roads Congress, "pedestrian encompasses all sets of people in the public domain irrespective of their age and (dis)abilities" (IRC, 2012).

Walking encompasses the whole gamut of mobility patterns made on foot that vary depending on purpose, destination and other factors. Walking may be a dynamic pedestrian behaviour viz. walking, playing, running, jogging, strolling or a static pedestrian activity viz. sitting, standing or socializing. Walking pace can vary across a spectrum of slow to vigorous. The pedestrian travel may be casual strolling trips around the neighbourhood or destination trips to work, recreation or shopping. Walking may be a mode of transport itself or an adjunct to other transport modes.

1.2   Walk-Friendly Traditional City Cores

Till the invention of motorised transport, human settlements catered primarily to the capabilities and limitations of a pedestrian; and were therefore compact, fine grained and had a size that could be easily traversed on foot. Towns of the medieval era still prevail in the cities that grew naturally over a period of time. These traditional city cores had a high cultural, aesthetic and historical significance. Quite invariably, a typical medieval character was echoed in these – *kuchas* and *galis*– narrow & winding streets often with dead ends, *mohallas* that represented the units of habitation, the main *bazaars* or the wider commercial streets forming the prime linkages of the outside to the focus of the settlement, which would inevitably be a religious institution or a royal palace, *chowks* as community spaces that figured as surprising open spaces, traditional specialized *bazaars*, shops/houses opening directly on to the streets. Having been planned from the perspective of a pedestrian, these settlements emulated a spirit of compactness and containment which was further emphasized through their walled character. This human-centric approach of the traditional streets ensured a high level of social interaction and cultural exchange. All the main streets of the settlement would lead to a religious institution or a royal palace that acted as the nuclei. Such streets assumed a mixed-land-use character with shops opening to the streets. The unique texture of the city fabric, the humane and pedestrian spirits of the settlement, the beauty and richness of detailing of the structures, the enormous capital of buildings, the subtlety and variety of the activities and the warmth of human relationships they offered are some of the exceptional qualities of the medieval cores that are increasingly being recognized as irreplaceable by the modern man (Figure 1.1).

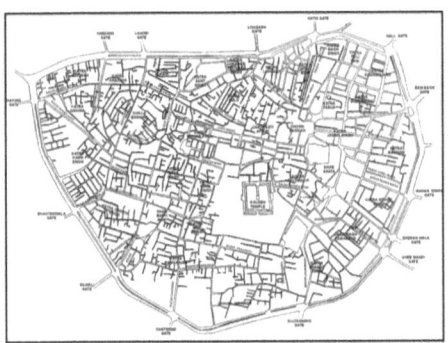 

Figure 1.1 Traditional city cores: Walled City, Amritsar, and Shahjahanabad, Delhi

1.3 Vehicle Invasion and the Pedestrian Narrative

Over the recent past, the cities across the world have witnessed a sharp increase in the auto ownership trends as also ever complicated mobility patterns. The modern society has increased its dependence on the private transport mode. In India, while the total registered vehicles grew at a compound annual growth rate or CAGR of 10.5 percent (Figure 1.2) between 2002 and 2012 (MoRTH, 2013), the modal split (Figure 1.3) revealed the largest share of 72.4 percent for the two-wheelers, followed by cars, jeeps and taxis having share of 13.5 percent with only 1.0 percent share for buses. Since the road capacities have not increased correspondingly, the limited road infrastructure bear the burden of escalated transport-related demands. This has literally choked our cities. The cities have become hostile, dirty, dangerous, unhealthy and insecure places to live. Various issues and grave concerns have emerged that question the sustainability and liveability of our cities in the contemporary times.

4 Towards Pedestrian-Friendly Neighbourhoods

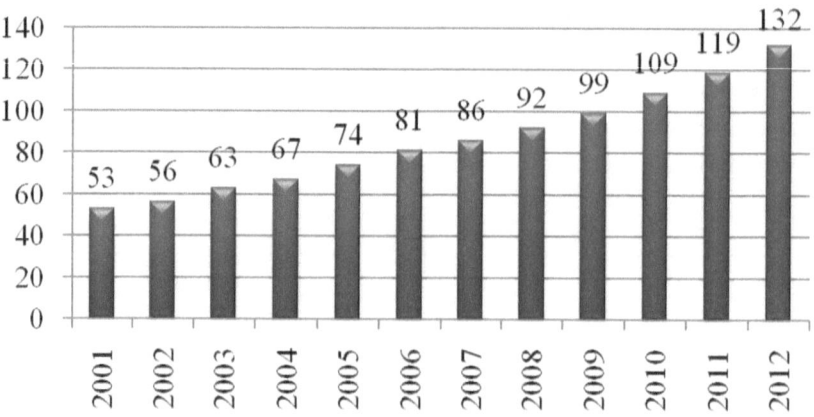

Figure 1.2 Registered vehicles per 1000 population in India [*Source*: MoRTH, 2013]

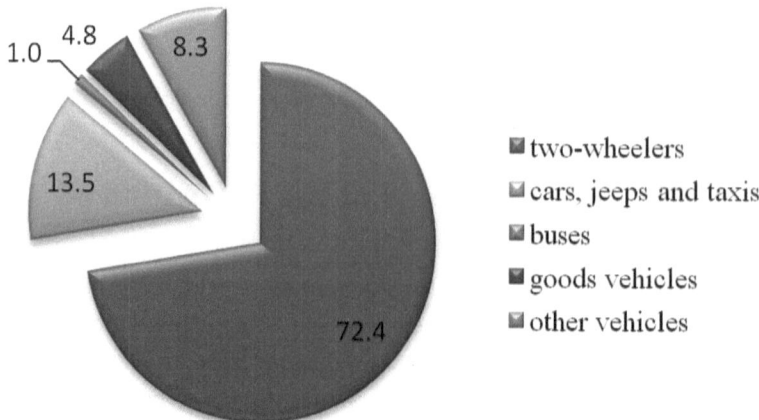

Figure 1.3 Modal split of registered vehicles (percent) for the year 2012 [*Source*: MoRTH, 2013]

Increased vehicular traffic has caused acute congestion on the roads severely impeding the mobility and accessibility of the pedestrians, cyclists and the disabled while challenging our road safety measures. The environmental consequences in terms of air and noise pollution are equally severe. In urban India, the transport sector is considered the major contributor to air pollution. As per a study of Delhi by the Central Pollution Control Board, India, 76.2 percent of carbon monoxide, 96.9 percent of hydrocarbons and 48.6 percent of nitrogen oxides in air are contributed by the transport sector (CSE, 2009). The level of suspended particulate matter in all metropolitan cities exceeds the limit set by the World Health Organization (Singh, 2005). Increased traffic congestion causes reduced vehicle speeds that drastically increase the level of vehicular emission. Transport, being wholly dependent on fossil fuel, contributes to global warming in a larger way. Transport has also impacted upon the cityscape and physical growth patterns. It has facilitated the decentralization of cities that spread much beyond their edges, causing substantial growth in trip lengths and development of dispersed travel patterns.

The current mobility trends and the consequent impacts on liveability, environment and physical growth patterns have adversely affected the pedestrian culture of our Indian cities. Various physical and social factors have connived jointly towards disappearance of the pedestrians from the urban scene.

- *Physical deterrents to walking*: The physical barriers or deterrents on the roads have since long evoked, across most societies, negative perceptions of walking as a mode of transport. However, the response to these worries has hardly been to check the traffic volume and speed. Rather the pedestrians have been forced to withdraw from the roads to avoid any casualties or accidents. Though a significant number of trips in Indian cities are made on foot (16–58 percent), pedestrian remains the neglected road user in terms of required infrastructure, amenities and services. Only about 30 percent of the roads in most Indian cities provide for pedestrian footpaths; and almost 20 percent of road accidents involve pedestrians (MoUD, 2008). Growing vehicular trends have also propagated dispersed patterns of activity and the lengthier journeys, creating destinations beyond reasonable walking distances. The distance over which walking may be considered feasible varies considerably, depending on the physical characteristics of pedestrian system, the pedestrians themselves and the purpose and context of the journey. However, 1–2 km has generally been regarded as an acceptable average distance in literature (Goodman and Tolley, 2003).
- *Social construction of transport*: Choice of the transport mode has often been viewed in relation to the social norms and culturally

shared perceptions, making it difficult to adopt behaviour outside this mainstream. Car travel assumes substantial social superiority in attributes such as status, wealth and power in addition to fulfilling its transport function. Social acceptability of walking has been grossly marginalized by cultural dominance of car. Walking, cycling and public transport are often equated with low social status. Further, the perceived scarcity of time is often forwarded as an excuse for resorting to the other transport modes in the modern society (Goodman and Tolley, 2003).

- *Invisibility of pedestrian in the past transport policies:* For a long time, urban roads in India have remained guided by the Codes of Practice issued by the Indian Roads Congress (IRC) as early as 1970s and 1980s. These codes and eventually the traditional traffic engineering practices have remained vehicle-centric. Walking has remained almost invisible in our urban and transport planning policies. Large proportion of modal share particularly for short journeys has often been overlooked. Issues of the pedestrians have never been collected at sufficiently detailed level that remained poorly represented. Reason for this neglect, as quoted by various scholars, is the *'universal'* and *'ordinary'* nature of walking. It has remained so basic to all planning and transport activities and so undemanding in terms of government finances that it always remained hidden and slipped through the net in strategy formulation. Little economic significance meant little economic incentive to plan for walking. Further, it offered no technological or engineering challenge to stimulate the planners. Being so omnipresent, it could not gather any powerful lobbies or advocacy groups. Therefore, the lack of professional focus compounded by failure of public to bring it to the attention of planners and politicians has ultimately led to the present unconcern.

1.4 Current Pedestrian Scenario in the Indian Cities

In 2008, Ministry of Urban Development, Government of India, carried out a national level survey for the purpose of formulating traffic and transportation-related policies and strategies in the urban areas of India. Thirty sample cities were shortlisted based on various factors such as size, shape, availability of public transport, economic activity, congestion and geographical location. These were surveyed to understand the existing transport scenario in India. In addition to several important aspects of traffic and transportation, the study also investigated walking trends and patterns in these 30 cities (MoUD, 2008). Various parameters like number of walk trips, trip lengths, walkability index, congestion, etc., were considered in relation to the size of the cities (Table 1.1). A *walk trip* considered the complete journey through stages from origin to final destination. In case of multiple modes in a single trip, the predominant mode was considered. *Trip length* considered the average distance travelled during a trip, and was calculated as the ratio of total passenger kilometre to the total number of trips. *Walkability index* evaluated the performance of pedestrian infrastructure based on the availability of foot path on major corridors and overall facility rating by pedestrians (MoUD, 2008).

The study revealed a considerable share of walk trips in all cities. With the exception of hill cities, walk trips in other Indian cities ranged from 16 to 46 percent of the daily trips. While Panaji, Pondicherry, Bikaner, Raipur and Madurai had walk trips exceeding 30 percent, only two cities namely Kolkata and Kochi had walk share less than 20 percent that was probably due to higher patronage of public transport in these two cities. Trip length was found to be directly related to the city size. Gangtok had the minimum trip length of 2.1 km, while Mumbai was identified with the maximum trip length of 11.9 km. About 24 cities had average trip length of a value less than 6 km. Chandigarh was found to have the highest walkability index, reflecting its better pedestrian facilities. Larger cities generally had higher walkability index though this too was embarrassingly short when compared to that of the cities of developed countries such as London that had walkability index of 1.5 to 1.7 as per rough estimates (MoUD, 2008). Average index for all cities together was found to be 0.52. Walkability index values for the small- and medium-sized cities were found to be lesser than the national average, signifying the need to enhance pedestrian facilities in these cities.

Table 1.1 Population-based walkability data for selected Indian cities

	Cities	Population in 2001 (lakhs)	Walk trips (percent)	Trip length (km)	Walkability index
1	Gangtok	0.92	56	2.1	0.30
2	Panaji	0.97	34	2.4	0.32
3	Shimla	1.73	58	3.0	0.22
4	Pondicherry	5.08	40	3.0	0.37
5	Bikaner	6.40	46	2.6	0.43
6	Raipur	7.19	35	3.0	0.41
7	Bhubaneswar	8.44	28	3.9	0.28
8	Chandigarh	9.66	23	4.5	0.91
9	HubliDharward	9.68	23	3.9	0.39
10	Guwahati	10.60	21	4.1	0.39
11	Amritsar	10.85	27	4.5	0.31
12	Trivandrum	11.22	26	4.7	0.34
13	Madurai	11.85	34	5.2	0.40
14	Agra	13.69	27	4.4	0.38
15	Bhopal	14.58	26	4.4	0.47
16	Kochi	18.18	16	5.5	0.57
17	Patna	18.36	26	4.5	0.65
18	Varanasi	18.95	24	4.9	0.33
19	Nagpur	21.13	21	5.0	0.66
20	Jaipur	26.80	26	6.0	0.64
21	Kanpur	27.16	29	5.6	0.59
22	Surat	30.90	27	6.0	0.62
23	Pune	42.00	22	6.1	0.81
24	Ahmedabad	59.34	22	6.2	0.85
25	Hyderabad	63.83	22	7.9	0.68
26	Chennai	70.14	22	8.6	0.77
27	Bangalore	86.25	26	9.6	0.63
28	Delhi	138.50	21	10.2	0.87
29	Kolkata	147.38	19	10	0.81
30	Mumbai	177.02	27	11.9	0.85

[*Source*: MoUD, 2008]

1.5 Discourses on Walking: Merely a Fad or a Worldwide Necessity

Currently, walking has become an essential ingredient of all global discourses on sustainable development. *Walk-friendly, walkability, pedestrian-sensitive* are certain expressions that reflect the desperation of modern society to counter the evils of ever-increasing motorised transport modes and return to more humane way of life. The advantages of walking in terms of environment, health, socio-cultural ties and overall economy, as discussed underneath, are projected equivocally by the various stakeholders of development.

- *Environmental reasons*: Congestion, crawling traffic and high pollution levels have made cities unliveable. Explosive numbers of vehicles and increased driving distances are provoking adverse climatic impacts. It is destined to get a lot worse if vehicle numbers continue to increase and the transport infrastructure remains focused to satiate the private transport only. Walking, on the other hand, is inherently eco-friendly and does not consume fuel. The green mode of transport reduces congestion and makes the least negative impact on environment in terms of air and noise pollution. Walking enhances liveability of the urban environment.
- *Health benefits*: Walking signifies the most basic form of physical activity. Health studies demonstrate that walking can promote mental and physical health including cardio-vascular fitness, reduced stress, stronger bones, mental alertness and creativity. It helps in prevention and control of some non-communicable diseases like diabetes, obesity, hypertension, cardiac problems and others.
- *Socio-cultural benefits*: Walking can be more than a purely utilitarian mode of travel for trips to work, school or shopping, and can have both social and recreational value. It strengthens social and community ties, and encourages a sense of pride in local environments. It forms an integral part of our customs and traditions, and therefore has an immense historical and cultural context. Walking, as an activity accessible to all social groups, age groups, religions and cultures, also ensures social equity.

- *Overall economy:* Walking benefits the local community in terms of economic stability. When communities relate strongly to the local environment and its unique culture, they develop a strong social capital of networks and trust that forms the basis of a robust urban economy. Further, walking is economical costing much less than the auto and public transport, both in terms of direct-user costs as also public infrastructure costs.

1.6 Visibility of Pedestrian in the Emerging Urban Planning and Design Movements

Human beings have time and again attempted to consciously and subconsciously plan theirsettlements while responding to the emerging needs and challenges of time and place. Traditional settlements, focused around a pedestrian,were characterized by a small, dense environment, often walled and generally not being much more than 5 kilometers from one end to the other. This form developed because of the need for all destinations to be within a reasonable walking distance. Industrial Revolution was a major development that caused unprecedented influx of people to the cities consequently makingthem ugly places to live in. This heralded an era of urban decentralization that caused millions of city dwellers to move away from the polluted downtown areas of industrializing cities to newly created suburbs. The proliferation of automobile in the early 20th century triggered and facilitated further decentralization or urban sprawl. At present, this dramatic increase in the number of vehicles on roads has brought in urban crisis since the prevalent models of development are proving inappropriate and deficient. Sustainability concerns have erupted finding voice in the name of environmental degradation, loss of community, social unrest, health concerns and so on. The emerging sustainability-related issues of the contemporary times have kicked off new and innovative planning concepts and approaches that are being tested in various countries. Having realized the importance of walking in the current scenario, these new approaches are consciously and proactively endorsing the pedestrian presence in the urban realm. As discussed underneath, these newly propagated urban forms and planning approaches have 'pedestrian' as an inevitable ingredient.

Compact city: *Compactcity* or *city of short distances* is an urban planning and design concept that promotes relatively high residential density with mixed land uses. It is based on an efficient public transport system and has an urban layout which – according to its advocates – encourages walking and cycling, low energy consumption and reduced pollution. However, achieving a *compact city* does not just mean increasing urban density per se or across all parts of the city; it means good planning to achieve an overall more compact urban form. It may be achieved by limiting outward urban expansion combined with efficient usage of land resources within its boundaries. Although the concept of *compact city* was coined by American writers, it has been used more in recent years by European and particularly British planners and academics.

The Netherlands' urban planning is highly influenced by the *compact city* concept. In the 1960s, cities expanded in large top-down planned neighbourhoods using the limited available space as efficiently as possible. Any further physical expansion of the city was prohibited giving way to the commuter towns at moderate distances from the main city. However, in the 1980s, it was realised that people preferred to live in the previously existing settlements, therefore new urban neighbourhoods were cleverly designed around these as outer skin. As a consequence of this, all neighbourhoods in Dutch towns are close to city centres, made relatively dense and with very good connections enabling inhabitants to get downtown by public transport or bicycle. This ensured a cleaner rural landscape while the cities were dense and compact.

New urbanism: *New urbanism* is an urban design movement which promotes environment-friendly habits by creating walkable neighbourhoods containing a wide range of housing and job types. The movement arose in the United States in the early 1980s, and spans a number of different disciplines and geographic scales. The organizing body for *new urbanism* – Congress for the New Urbanism (CNU) – was founded in 1993. *New urbanism* principles have become increasingly influential in the fields of planning, architecture and public policy; and advocate the restructuring of public policy and development practices to support the following principles:

- Neighbourhoods should be diverse in use and population.
- Communities should be designed for the pedestrian and transit as well as the car.

- Cities and towns should be shaped by physically defined and universally accessible public spaces and community institutions.
- Urban places should be framed by architecture and landscape design that celebrate local history, climate, ecology and building practice.

Based on the principles of how cities and towns had been built for the last several centuries, *new urbanism* focuses on human-scaled urban design. The principles may be applied to new development, urban infill and revitalization, and preservation. They can be applied to all scales of development in the full range of places including rural main streets, booming suburban areas, urban neighbourhoods, dense city centres, and even entire regions.

Several terms are viewed as synonymous, included in, or overlapping with the *new urbanism: neo-traditional development, traditional neighbourhood development, traditional urbanism, walkable urbanism, transit-oriented development, liveable communities* and *new pedestrianism*.

Transit-oriented development: In urban planning, a *transit-oriented development* (TOD) is a type of urban development that maximizes the amount of residential, business and leisure space within walking distance of public transport. In doing so, TOD aims to increase public transport ridership by reducing the use of private cars and by promoting sustainable urban growth. A TOD typically includes a central transit stop (such as a train station, or light rail or bus stop) surrounded by a high-density mixed-use area, with lower-density areas spreading out from this centre. A TOD is also typically designed to be more walkable than other built-up areas, through using smaller block sizes and reducing the land area dedicated to automobiles. The densest areas of a TOD are normally located within a radius of ¼ to ½ mile (400 to 800 m) around the central transit stop, as this is considered to be an appropriate scale for pedestrians, thus solving the last mile problem.

Many of the new towns created after World War II in Japan, Sweden and France have many of the characteristics of TOD communities. In a sense, nearly all communities built on reclaimed land in the Netherlands or as exurban developments in Denmark have had the local equivalent of TOD principles integrated in their planning, including the promotion of bicycles for local use. In the United States, a half-mile-radius circle has become the de-facto standard for rail-transit catchment areas for TODs.

A half mile (800 m) corresponds to the distance someone can walk in 10 minutes at 3 mph (4.8 km/h) and is a common estimate for the distance people will walk to get to a rail station.

Traditional neighbourhood development: Traditional neighbourhood development (also called *neo-traditional development* or *urban village development* or simply TND) refers to the development of a complete neighbourhood or town using traditional town planning principles; the concept originated in the United States in 1990 in the Town of Bedford, New Hampshire. TND calls for compact, pedestrian-oriented neighbourhoods with a mix of commercial and residential uses, a variety of housing types, and public places where people have opportunities to socialize and engage in civic life. The automobile is still accommodated, with ample parking and efficient circulation, but it no longer dominates the landscape.

Figure 1.4 Example of Traditional Neighbourhood Development. The 1986 plan for Mashpee Commons helped convert an old shopping centre (at left) into a mixed-use New England village. [*Source*: CRCOG Best Practices Manual]

TND revisits many features of urban neighbourhoods developed before World War II, the single most distinguishing feature of which is the continuous fabric of intimately blended and mixed land uses arranged so that travel between them can be made by a variety of methods in addition to the usual private automobile. Mashpee Commons is one of the most successful examples of TND in the United States. In 1986, this former disinvested strip mall in Mashpee, Massachusetts, was converted into Mashpee Commons, a mixed-use, mixed-income, pedestrian-friendly town centre. The plan was so successful that five residential neighbourhoods, all in a TND format, were planned around the Commons (Figure 1.4).

New pedestrianism:*New pedestrianism* is supposedly a more pedestrian and ecology-oriented variation of *new urbanism* in urban planning theory, founded in 1999 by Michael E. Arth, an American artist, urban/home/landscape designer, futurist and author. A neighbourhood or new town utilizing *new pedestrianism* is called a *pedestrian village*. *Pedestrian villages* can range from being nearly car-free to having automobile access behind nearly every house and business, but pedestrian lanes are always in front. By eliminating the front street and replacing it with a tree-lined pedestrian lane, emphasis is placed on walking and cycling. Pedestrian lanes are usually 12–15 feet (5 m) wide, with one smooth side for rolling conveyances such as bicycles, skates,etc., and the other, narrower, textured side for pedestrians and wheelchairs. Eliminating the automobile street from the front allows for intimate scale plazas, fountains, pocket parks, as well as an unspoiled connection to natural features such as lakes, streams and forests that may border or be included in a *pedestrian village*. A vast public realm is created that is free from the sight, smell and sound of automobiles, while the automobiles are still served on a separate network. In 2005 *new pedestrianism* was offered by Arth as part of the solution to the rebuilding of New Orleans.

1.7 Conclusion

It becomes clear that the pedestrian culture that pervades through all the sections of the society is getting threatened and may vanish in the today's automobile dependant societies. This realisation is growing, and therefore, concerted efforts are required by all the stakeholders of development to address the emergent need of the present times.

References

- CSE (2009). *Footfalls: Obstacle Course to Livable Cities.* Centre for Science and Environment, Delhi. <http://www.cseindia.org/userfiles/walkability_pdf.pdf>
- Goodman, R., andTolley, R. (2003). The decline of everyday walking in the UK: Explanations and policy implications. *Sustainable Transport: Planning for Walking and Cycling in Urban Environments.* Rodney Tolley (ed). Woodland Publishing Limited, England.
- IRC (2012). *Guidelines for Pedestrian Facilities (First Revision).* Indian Roads Congress.IRC:103-2012.
- MoRTH (2013). *Road Transport Year Book (2011-12).* Ministry of Road Transport & Highways, Government of India, New Delhi.
- MoUD (2008). *Study on Traffic and Transportation Policies and Strategies in Urban Areas in India.* Prepared by Wilbur Smith Associates for the Ministry of Urban Development, Government of India, New Delhi.
- NZ Transport Agency (2008). *Pedestrian Planning and Design Guide.* New Zealand.
- Singh, S.K. (2005). Review of urban transportation in India. *Journal of Public Transportation* 8(1):79-97.

Websites

- https://en.wikipedia.org/wiki/Compact_city
- https://en.wikipedia.org/wiki/New_Urbanism
- https://en.wikipedia.org/wiki/Transit-oriented_development
- https://everipedia.org/wiki/New_pedestrianism/

2
In Quest for the Pedestrian Revival

The chapter explores the suitability and feasibility of injecting pedestrian spirits in the urban realm. In this regard, various factors that may influence the pedestrian attitudes and frequencies are explored with special emphasis on the role of built environment. Neighbourhoods are projected as the most suitable city modules for promoting walk spirits in the daily lives of people across all the sections of society. Efforts in various cities across the globe in terms of various policies and practices build up a strong case for promoting pedestrian spirits in the Indian cities.

2.1 What Determines the Walk Behaviour?

Walking, much like any other human behaviour, is largely influenced by individual circumstances, preferences and characteristics as also by socio-cultural and environmental factors (Mehta, 2008; Figure 2.1). *Individual factors* are shaped by considerations like age, gender, income, car ownership, household status, ethnicity, educational level, etc. The economic status too determines the fondness or disdain for walking. *Socio-cultural factors* include the general attitude of the society towards motorized or non-motorized transport, perception of local neighbourhoods, social relationships and traditional values. *Environment* may further be considered as *natural* and *built*. While the *natural environment* comprises the macro and micro-climatic conditions, the *built environment* is repeatedly being highlighted in the planning literature in terms of its six dimensions: residential density, street connectivity, accessibility to destinations (land-use mix diversity), walking and cycling environment, aesthetic quality and safety from traffic and crime (Clifton et al., 2007).

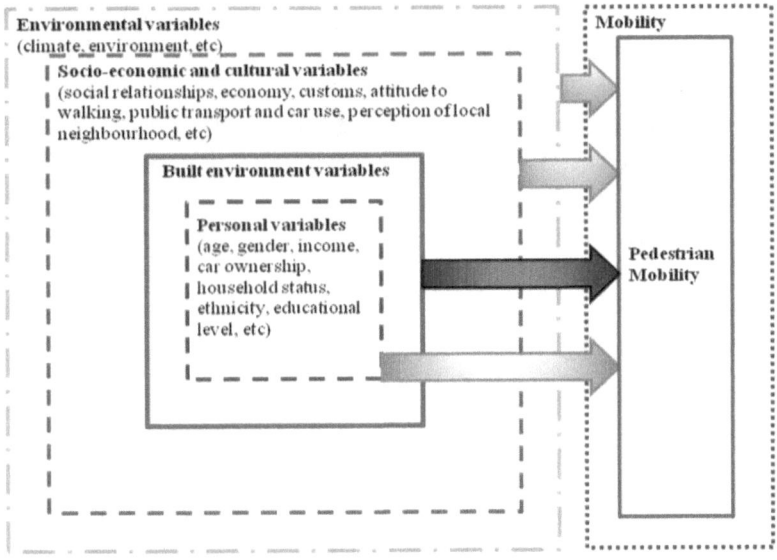

Figure 2.1 Variables impacting on pedestrian mobility

A pedestrian has several expectations from the built environment influencing his decision to walk. Alfonzo et al. (2008) forwarded a hierarchy of walking needs while reproducing the Maslow's hierarchy of human needs indicating that certain aspects of the built environment matter more than the others. These are *accessibility, safety and security, comfort* and *attractiveness or pleasurability*.

- *Accessibility* refers to the extent of connectivity (short and direct routes, compact urban fabric, etc.) to key attractors like public transport interchanges, homes, places of work and leisure destinations.
- *Safety and security* requires a legible environment with ability to see and understand the surroundings, visibility to other pedestrians, and alternative routes to avoid potentially threatening situations.
- *Comfort* emerges out of the facilities enroute like benches, litter bins, water, etc., and; shelters from inclement weather, shaded paths, etc.
- *Attractiveness or pleasurability* requires a clean pollution-free environment with exciting things to look at while walking; as also human activity, social interaction and sense of belongingness.

While accessibility and safety concerns are vital for the basic decision to walk, the general attractiveness of the surroundings and availability of comforts and conveniences enroute may enhance the walking experience. As per Alfonzo et al. (2008), the latter would not be considered for the decision to walk unless the former are met to a satisfactory extent. The knowledge of relative importance becomes particularly significant when making decisions concerning design or planning interventions intended to increase walking.

2.2   Neighbourhood as an Urban Planning Module

The neighbourhood as a unit is a ubiquitous phenomenon in every urban and non-urban area. In its purest definition, a neighbourhood is the vicinity in which people live. Lewis Mumford presented 'neighbourhood' as a 'fact of nature', which comes into existence whenever a group of people share a place. Since the coining of the expression 'neighbourhood unit' in 1929 by Clarence A. Perry, a New York planner, it has become a recurring theme in planning our cities (Gallion and Eisner, 1984). The concept propagated by Clarence A. Perry (Figure 2.2) was carried forward by N. L. Engelhardt, Jr., Clarence Stein and several other thinkers with certain variations or elaborations. The term has been defined and redefined throughout the planning history. Despite several variations, the principle of neighbourhood unit represents a unit of the population with basic common needs for educational, recreational and other service facilities; and it is the standards for these facilities from which the size and design of the neighbourhood emerge. Whittick (1974) describes neighbourhood unit as "an integrated, planned urban area related to the larger community of which it is a part and consisting of residential districts, a school or schools, shopping facilities, religious buildings, open spaces, and perhaps a degree of service industry".

In the current context, however, the term has lost its initial significance though it persists being frequently referred to in the context of traditional and contemporary residential developments. The contemporary planning practices visualize a city as a living organism made up of cells. This allows easy comprehension of its vast and shapeless expanse. This basic cellular notion gets reinforced, in the case of residential areas, by the notion

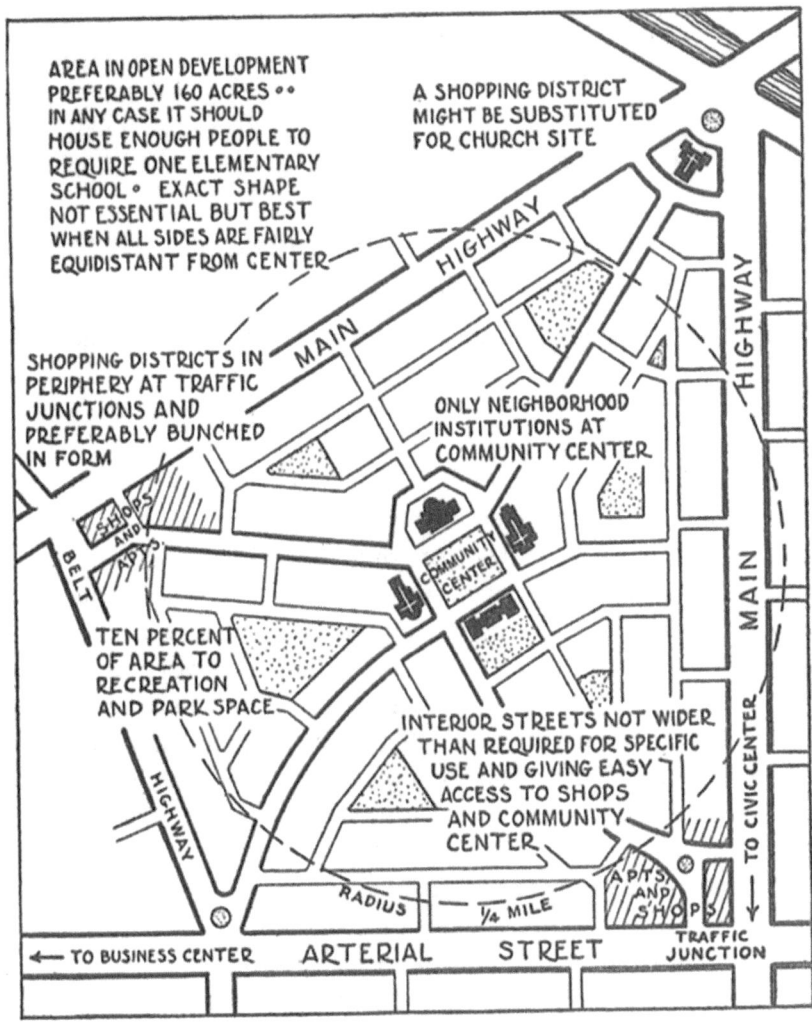

Figure 2.2 Clarence A. Perry's Neighbourhood Unit of 1929

of neighbourhood (Lynch, 1984). Further, planning has traditionally demanded a de-centralized, participatory planning process to successfully address local issues. Neighbourhood, as a unit of planning, has always provided organizations the means to apply planning processes and implement local planning programs and policies at the desirable de-centralized level. In the minds of most people as well, neighbourhood is a popular and accepted element of social and physical organization. Further, influenced by the awakening of neo-traditionalism as paradigm for urban living, sense of neighbourhood has become the core concept through which neighbourhood attachment and communality are being evaluated (Horn, 2004).

2.3 Appropriateness of Neighbourhoods for Promoting Pedestrian Culture

Walking is increasingly being valued within short distance range of 1-2 km. A large number of people access essential services like education, local shopping, leisure trips within neighbourhoods and job centres. However, people increasingly rely on motorized modes within this short distance range due to hostile walking conditions. Therefore the neighbourhood, representing an area whereby the daily needs of the residents must be addressed within short distance range without compromising upon the safety and security of its inhabitants, must offer an environment that essentially relates to the pace and scale of a pedestrian (Figure 2.3 and 2.4). It is realised that the physical extent of neighbourhoods along with their administrative status and fairly uniform socio-cultural characteristics offer them to be the most suitable modules for promoting pedestrian culture in the society. In India, the sensitivity towards pedestrian concerns is getting evident in the urban planning and transport policies though in a lukewarm manner. The efforts, in most instances, are focused at segment level or at the comprehensive city level. Potential of neighbourhoods for promoting walk culture among residents in the Indian cities need to be realised and promoted.

Figure 2.3 Desirable modal preference in a metropolitan city

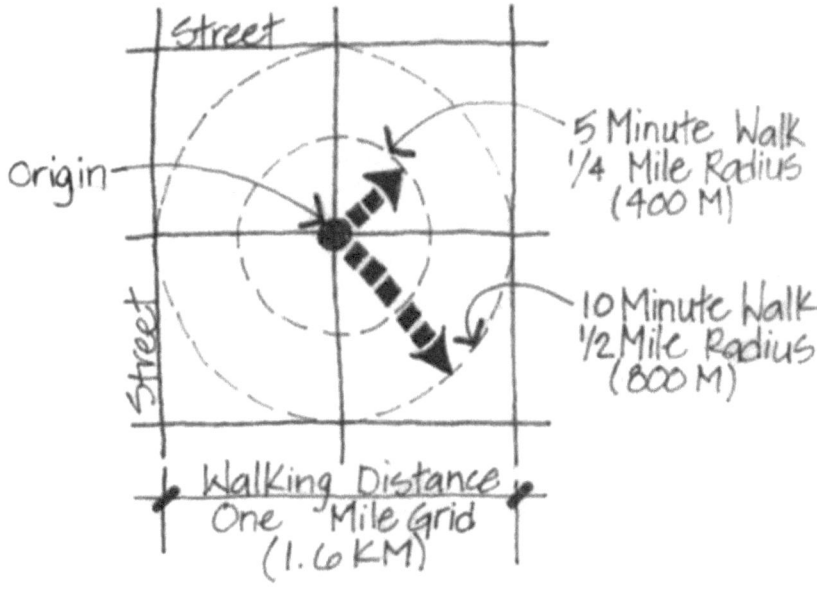

Figure 2.4 Average walking distance [*Source*: MAoG, 2005]

2.4 Impact of the Built Environment on Pedestrian Mobility

The cumulative impact of various aspects of built environment on the pedestrian's choice or decision to walk determines the walkability. Despite being highly subjective, walkability serves as a useful tool to assess the characteristics of an area or a route for pedestrian studies. Several studies were attempted to congregate and consolidate the built environment features that may have marked influence on the walkability of neighbourhoods. However, ambiguity still prevails as regards the exact relation of various factors to the pedestrian mobility as also their relative importance. Ewing (2000) prepared a comprehensive list of features important for 'pedestrian-friendly environment' categorizing them as essential, highly desirable or nice additions. The variables and indicators of the built environment that are often associated with pedestrian mobility patterns, in literature, are discussed hereafter (Ewing, 2000; Talen, 2002; GDOT, 2003; and NZ Transport Agency, 2008) (Table 2.1). These are also discussed elsewhere (Singhal and Chahal, 2015).

Table 2.1 Variables and indicators of built environment determining pedestrian mobility

	Built Environment Variables	Indicators
1	Neighbourhood density and layout	1. Population density 2. Accessibility to facilities 3. Connectivity and permeability 4. Block length and street network 5. Land-use mix
2	Spatial quality and configuration of streets	1. Street-oriented buildings 2. Visual enclosure 3. Parking provision, design and control 4. Street trees and landscaping
3	Street geometry, amenities and materials	1. Sidewalks and street crossings 2. Pedestrian amenities 3. Signage and public art 4. Street lighting 5. Surface materials

2.4.1 Neighbourhood density and layout

Population density: Higher population densities of the neighbourhoods signify more people in the public domain, meaning thereby more active and lively street life, informal surveillance and security of the public realm, viable neighbourhood businesses, more residents within walking distance of transit stops, and a consequent greater inclination to walk or use transit. Densities at the ground floor level would be of a better consequence. High densities achieved through small plot sizes enhance walking more than high-rise constructions which are often associated with their socially alienating effects due to lower densities at ground floor levels (Ewing, 2000).

Accessibility to facilities: Accessibility refers to the ability to reach a given destination based on geographic distance (Talen, 2002), and forms the basic criterion for a person's decision to walk. People are more likely to walk when they have their destination located in close proximity. While different pedestrians would have different physical and cognitive abilities, these do not remain constant even for a particular pedestrian; and would rather change during different journeys or even during the same walk journey as he becomes tired or acquires some load to carry. Acceptable walking distances will vary depending on the trip purpose, weather and time of day, geography, demographics and several other factors (WSDT,

1997). Most people will walk longer distances for recreational purposes as compared to work or education related journeys when they are in a hurry. "Most people will walk ¼ mile (0.4 km), or approximately 1,400 feet (427 m) with one mile (1.6 km) as the maximum distance of a walking trip" (MAoG, 2005). The vast majority of people walk at speeds between 2.9 km/h and 6.5 km/h with average being 5.4 km/h. The limit of 1/4th mile is considered a comfortable walking distance for local access to community facilities, neighbourhood parks and other popular pedestrian destinations because of its wider acceptance in planning literature (NZ Transport Agency, 2008).

Connectivity and permeability: Connectivity and permeability describe the extent to which urban forms permit or restrict the movement of people or vehicles in different directions. As per Stephen Marshall, connectivity refers solely to the number of connections to and from a particular land use parcel or activity location within an area, whereas permeability describes the capacity of those connections to carry people or vehicles (Figure 2.5). Permeable networks encourage walking and cycling, and make places easier to steer through. However, over-provision of poorly used permeability (e.g. rear alleyways) is a crime hazard and can lead to problems of anti-social behaviour.

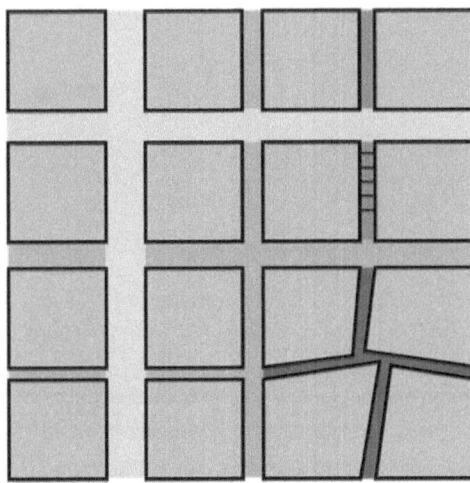

Equally connected, streets become less permeable to motorized transport from light to dark gray

Figure 2.5 Image depicting distinction between connectivity and permeability
[*Source*: https://en.wikipedia.org/wiki/Permeability]

Two streams of thought are identified in this context. As per the proponents of filtered permeability or segregation-oriented perspective, the networks for walking and cycling should be more permeable than the road network for motor vehicles, thus offering them time and convenience advantage over car driving. Contradicting this viewpoint is the unfiltered permeability or interaction-oriented perspective, the central principle of new urbanism that favours urban designs based upon the traditional or mixed-use streets, where pedestrians, cyclists and motor vehicles follow the same routes. Fostering interactions between motorized modes and pedestrians is assumed to be the key to achieving sustainable mobility patterns.

Certain European cities such as Freiburg, and its rail suburb Vauban and Groningen have achieved high levels of walking and cycling by following principles of filtered permeability, sometimes described as 'a coarse grain for cars and a fine grain for cyclists and pedestrians' (Figure 2.6).

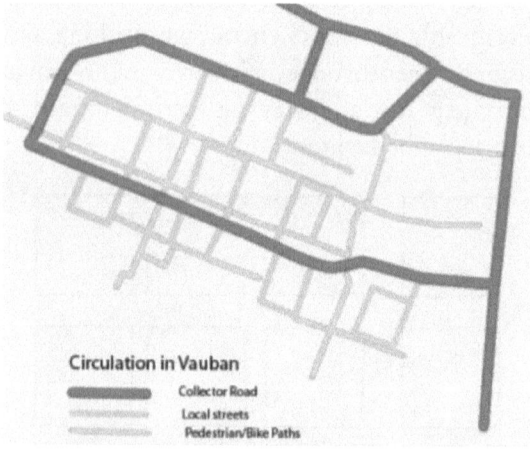

Figure 2.6 Diagrammatic depiction of transportation network in Vauban, Freiburg, Germany [*Source*: https://en.wikipedia.org/wiki/Permeability]

Block length and street network: The trend towards longer blocks and correspondingly fewer intersections has contributed to a city scaled to automobile. Short blocks and frequent cross streets allow for relatively more direct routing for the pedestrians (Parks and Schofer, 2006). This offers more route choices making the walk more eventful. Frequent intersections shorten the sense of elapsed time on walk trips. As per

Ewing (2000), for a high degree of walkability, block lengths of about 300 feet are desirable; blocks of 400–500 feet too work well; but as blocks grow to 600–800 feet, adjacent blocks become isolated from each other.

Street grids, though promoting higher vehicular speeds, generally allow better pedestrian circulation because they have more intersections and more connecting streets. Curved or irregular streets contribute to variety and a sense of place; may be appropriate in case of topographical or other site constraints. However, layouts that use excessive or gratuitous curves are less efficient and make access for pedestrians more difficult (Figure 2.7).

Street grids create potential for direct routing that is important to pedestrians.

Layouts with many cul-de-sacs make access for pedestrians more difficult.

Figure 2.7 Impact of street networks on pedestrians [*Source*: NZ Transport Agency, 2008]

Land-use Mix: Mixing of compatible land uses increases the likelihood that a desired destination is nearby in the neighbourhood thus making it accessible on foot. Mixed uses attract different people at different times for different purposes that make for a lively public realm resulting in greater personal security because of natural surveillance (Tibbalds, 2005). Single dominant land-use produces clientele with similar schedules viz. mothers in mid-afternoon or office workers at lunch time, leaving the spaces depopulated at other hours.

2.4.2 Spatial quality and configuration of streets

Street-oriented buildings: The way the street facades relate to the streets greatly determine the pedestrian behaviour. The buildings with their backs or blank sides on the street may define and enclose the space, but that space shall be unexciting (Figure 2.8). The building facades as also the spaces adjoining streets need to be sensitively treated to arouse pedestrian interest. Variety and detailing in architectural disposition, textural and colour treatments and accentuation through light-shade effects inject life into space and induce pedestrian curiosity. Visual penetrability of street facades especially at ground floor level creates pedestrian interest (Ewing and Handy, 2009). Accordingly, the main entries shall face the street and significant number of windows shall open at street level. Commercial streets with see-through display windows and the residential streets with front porches or prominent front doors are attractive for walking. Inactive uses such as parking lots create dead street spaces.

Long visually impenetrable facades marginalize the pedestrians travelling at slow speeds
(*Photo courtesy*: Author)

Figure 2.8 Impact of street facades on pedestrians

Visual enclosure: Visual enclosure enhances 'place' function of the streets inviting more activity on the streets. While in an urban setting, enclosure is formed by lining the street or plaza with unbroken building fronts of roughly equal height; at low suburban densities, street trees assume the dominant role. Ewing (2000) considers height-to-width ratio of 1:6 as minimum and 1:3 as optimum for appropriate urban spatial definition. In general, the tighter the ratio, the stronger would be the sense of place (Figure 2.9). Unlike the solid enclosure of buildings, tree lines depend on visual suggestion and illusion. Street space will seem enclosed only if trees are closely spaced (Ewing and Handy, 2009). Visual enclosure is also created by properly scaled walls and fences as also the visual termination points at street ends viz. prominent buildings, monuments, fountains or other architectural elements. Enclosure is eroded by breaks in continuity in the vertical elements such as buildings or tree rows that line the street; or spaces occupied by inactive uses that do not generate human presence viz. vacant or parking lots, driveways, etc. Large building setbacks adversely affect the visual enclosure.

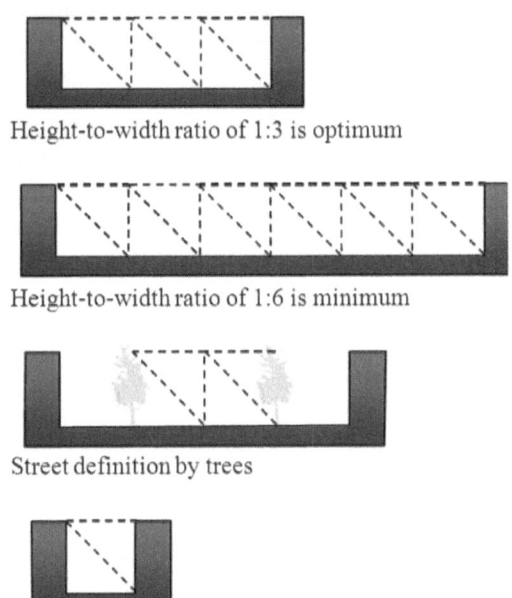

Figure 2.9 Visual enclosure for spatial definition [*Source*: DfT, 2007]

Parking provision, design and control: Parking lots are a major source of dead spaces in cities. On-street parking is often widely supported as it provides opportunities for people to access the sidewalk directly from their vehicles and increase street activity. However, the street that takes up a large amount of frontage for parking makes pedestrian access to buildings difficult (Parks and Schofer, 2006). In general, parked cars should not dominate the streetscape, and be better placed to the rear or side of buildings. Peter Calthorpe recommends that parking lots occupy no more than one-third of the frontage along pedestrian-oriented streets, and no more than 75 feet in a stretch (Ewing, 2000). Further, parking lots should be designed in close coordination with landscaping, pedestrian walkways and pedestrian amenities, such that large areas of asphalt are attractively broken up and a nice street edge is created.

Street trees and landscaping: Right trees planted at the right spacing and in the right locations contribute to nearly all pedestrian-friendly design objectives viz. comfort, safety, human scale, linkage, visual enclosure, complexity, coherence and sense of place (Figure 2.10). Right trees shall be the shady trees that will grow to 50–70 feet at maturity with canopy starting at 15 feet or so above the ground. While the constant movement of branches and leaves, and the ever changing patterns of light created, add to the visual complexity of the streetscape; low canopy contrasts with the monumentality of wide spaces and tall buildings, creating human scale within larger volumes. Right spacing, depending on the size of the tree at maturity, shall be 30 feet or lesser, and shall imply enough closeness to form a continuous canopy over the sidewalk and a buffer between street and sidewalk. Trees located between the street and the sidewalk offer physical and psychological barrier for the pedestrians. Trees visually limit street space, calm traffic and shade the entire right-of-way. Using low height shrubs and upward branching trees will maintain visibility and sight distance at intersections, driveways, crossings, and other critical areas along the street system. Planting buffers, positioned between walkways and streets, can be landscaped in a variety of ways to aesthetically enhance the street side environment (Ewing, 2000).

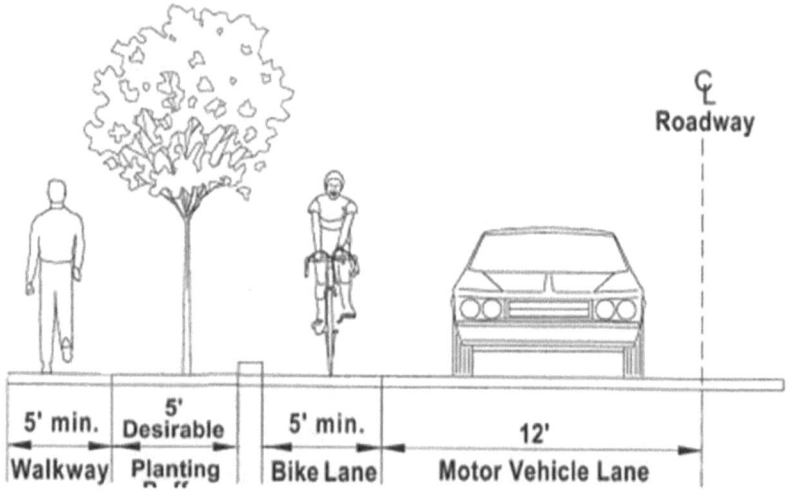

Trees located between the street and the sidewalk offer physical and psychological barrier for the pedestrians

Figure 2.10 Impact of right trees at the right location [Source: GDT, 2003]

2.4.3 Street geometry, amenities and materials

Sidewalks and street crossings: Sidewalks are typically raised and located adjacent to curbs or separated from the curb by a linear planting strip. Sidewalks need to be scaled to pedestrian traffic volumes. These need to be wide enough to accommodate pedestrian traffic, yet not be so wide as to appear empty most of the time. Sidewalks are typically 5 feet wide on local residential streets, and may even be 10, 15 or 20 feet for high pedestrian volumes (Ewing, 2000). Lack of sidewalks implies pedestrians must either walk on the roadway, which decreases safety; or walk alongside the road in an environment that may be muddy, rocky or have steep terrain (Parks and Schofer, 2006).

Most injuries and fatalities involving pedestrians occur as pedestrians attempt to cross streets. Richard Untermann, a leading authority on pedestrianisation, recommends marked crosswalks every 100 feet on pedestrian streets (Ewing, 2000). Striped crosswalks or zebra crossings provide safer crossings because they provide better visibility for both drivers and pedestrians. Street corners, when designed sharp rather than rounded, shorten crossing distances for pedestrians (Figure 2.11).

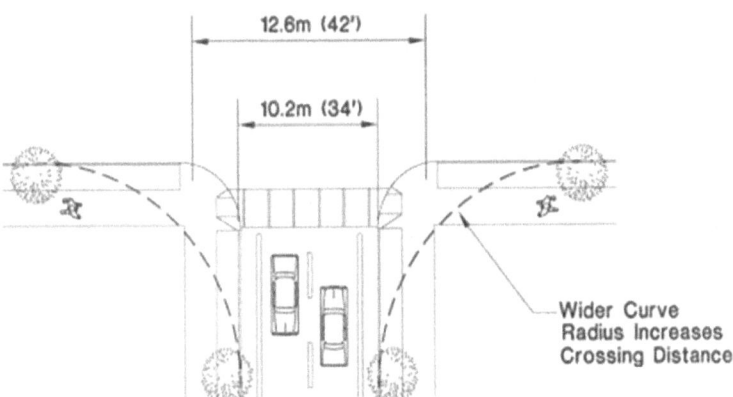

Figure 2.11 Impact of street corners on crossing distance [*Source*: NZ Transport Agency, 2008]

Pedestrian amenities: Through zoning and subdivision requirements, streets in residential areas can be designed with lighting, benches, trash containers and other amenities that are conducive to pedestrian activity. Waiting and resting areas along walkways provide welcome relief to pedestrians, particularly those who have mobility impairments, or lack stamina. Obstacles, such as sign posts, street furniture and utility facilities should be placed outside the main travel way used by pedestrians, in the fixtures/planting zone (Figure 2.12).

Figure 2.12 Placement of pedestrian amenities ideally in the fixture/planting zone
[*Source*: NZ Transport Agency, 2008]

Signage and public art: Signage and public art are a major source of complexity in the public realm. If well-coordinated, these may add visual quality to the street. Excessive and insensitive use may create visual clutter and physical obstacles. For the benefit of pedestrians, distances to identify key origins and destinations, average walking time and other meaningful information may be displayed on kiosks or other designated areas. Walking maps would ease way finding around a new urban environment. Signage should not protrude into the vertical clearance area (below 80 inches) of the entire public sidewalk.

Street lighting: Street lighting enhances pedestrian safety, security and comfort as also the economic vitality of urban area. Ample lighting allows pedestrians to be better seen by motorists at night; to see better and feel more secure during night-time hours; to read street name signs or to identify any obstacles in or near the sidewalk or path at night. Of the primary types of lighting available for pedestrian facilities viz. vapour lighting, high or low pressure sodium street lights, etc., the high pressure sodium street lights, in most cases, offer the most overall advantages when lighting the street area.

Surface materials: Materials used for pavement and amenities should be selected based on their colour, permeability, conductivity and emissivity as also the ease of maintenance. Lighter colour materials with low emissivity retain less heat and contribute to lowering the temperature in a space. Special areas may incorporate special paving, though sparingly being expensive, into the design of sidewalks and pedestrian areas for visual impacts. However, the bricks, cobbles, precast pavers and patterned concrete cannot compensate for otherwise poorly defined street space.

2.5 Global Policies for Promoting Walk Culture

Several governments across the globe have become proactive in addressing the pedestrian concerns, and have prepared and released manuals for consumption by the various stakeholders of development. Some of these are Pedestrian Facilities Guidebook by Department of Transportation, Washington State (1997), Portland Pedestrian Design Guide (1998), Florida Pedestrian Planning and Design Handbook (1999), Vermont Pedestrian and Bicycle Facility Planning and Design Manual (2002), Pedestrian and Streetscape Guide, Georgia (2003), A Guide to North Carolina Bicycle and Pedestrian Laws (2004), The Walking Plan for London (2004), Pedestrian Policies and Design Guidelines by Maricopa Association of Governments (2005), Manual for Streets for England by Transport for London (2007), Pedestrian Planning and Design Guide, New Zealand (2008), Complete Streets Design Guidelines (2009) by Knoxville Regional Transportation Planning Organization, San Francisco Better Streets Plan: Policies and Guidelines for the Pedestrian Realm (2010), Planning and Designing for Pedestrians: Guidelines for Western Australia (2012) and Street Design Manual by New York City Department of Transportation (2015). The subsequent sections bring forth excerpts from a few of these documents.

2.5.1 Pedestrian and Streetscape Guide, Georgia (2003)

With its mission to ensure a safe, efficient and sustainable transportation system for all users, Georgia State Department of Transportation released a 'Pedestrian and Streetscape Guide' for consumption by various agencies and professionals in its jurisdiction (GDOT, 2003). The document attempts to encourage pedestrian-centric approach through comprehensive land-use planning and in the provision of transportation facilities. A connected system of pedestrian routes is considered important. Transportation designs that accommodate pedestrian are understood to reinforce a sense of neighbourhood and community. Well-designed pedestrian facilities may complement local business activity and would enhance intermodal access for persons with impaired mobility. The document also emphasizes upon defining jurisdictional roles in providing pedestrian facilities. The document brings forth the typical elements of pedestrian-friendly streets, as follows (GDOT, 2003):

- Interconnectedness and small block patterns that facilitate the pedestrian access, mobility and safety
- Streets scaled down for pedestrians that discourage high vehicle speeds
- Traffic calming devices to reduce traffic speeds
- Median refuge islands to offer safe haven area to the pedestrians crossing the road
- Public spaces or pockets along the main pedestrian route as a place for pedestrians to rest and interact
- Awnings/covered building entrances that shelter pedestrians from adverse weather conditions
- Planting buffers with landscaping and street trees that provide shelter and shade without obstructing sight distances and help to soften the surrounding buildings and hard surfaces
- Street lighting designed to pedestrian scale
- Wide and continuous sidewalks or separated walkways that are fully accessible
- Clear delineation and direction for the pedestrians

2.5.2   The Walking Plan for London (2004)

'The Walking Plan for London' is based on the Mayor's vision of making London one of the world's most walking-friendly cities by 2015 (TfL, 2004). The Plan identifies various key issues relevant to walking in London and proposes how they can be addressed in a practical and cost effective way. 'The Walking Plan for London' sees more people making walking their first choice for short journeys and making more trips over longer distances by a combination of walking and public transport. The Plan supports the revitalisation of public spaces and the creation of a high quality urban environment that enriches Londoners' experience and appreciation of walking as a valued and enjoyable activity. Part 3 of the document sets out an Action Plan and suggests an approach to developing targets at local level. Actions are listed under six key objectives that focus upon: (1) improving co-ordination and inclusiveness in the delivery of Walking Plan; (2) promoting walking through public education and information utilizing published material and campaigns; (3) improving street conditions; (4) improving new developments and interchanges; (5) improving safety and security of pedestrians; and (6) timely delivery of the Plan and its monitoring (TfL, 2004).

The document also recommends taking inspiration from the cities that serve as examples of novel and ideal walking initiatives. Examples include Barcelona, Birmingham, Bristol, Lyon, Strasbourg, Freiburg, Copenhagen, Portland (Oregon) and Melbourne (TfL, 2004).

2.5.3 Manual for Streets, England (2007)

The Manual gives advice for the design of residential streets in England and Wales. It represents a strong Government and Welsh Assembly commitment to the creation of sustainable and inclusive public spaces. The Manual recognises five functions of streets – *place, movement, access, parking and provision for drainage, utilities and street lighting*. However, it is the *place function* that essentially distinguishes a street from a road, where the main purpose is to facilitate movement. The Manual introduces a user hierarchy in which pedestrians are considered first in the design process to ensure that all the user groups are properly considered at an early stage (DfT, 2007). The document proclaims as follows:
- The pedestrian routes shall be designed properly or else they would promote antisocial behaviour and crimes.
- Attractive and convenient walk environments enhance the vibrancy of the place and discourage reliance on motor transport.
- Good designs lead to high-quality attractive places that shall be socially, economically and environmentally sustainable.
- Street widths are crucial and must relate to building heights and the proposed characteristics of the streets.
- The buildings' fronts and backs shall be treated correctly in order to make streets work as places, and shall be guided by the basic tenet of *"public fronts and private backs"*

- Planting would be highly advantageous as they soften the urban street-scene, create visual and sensory interest and ameliorate the microclimate. These may be utilised to limit forward visibility thus checking the vehicle speeds.
- The design approach shall be all inclusive irrespective of age or physical ability. Designs that address the needs of children and disabled people shall be suitable for most users.
- Pedestrian paths shall be kept as straight as possible to minimise diversion from desire lines.
- The residential street design should inherently discourage high traffic speeds, without having to rely on vertical or horizontal deflection measures.
- Signage should be utilised sparingly only where it serves a clear function. The signage clutter shall generally be avoided.
- Lighting needs to be ample to encourage pedestrian activity while preventing crime. *"Reducing the height of lighting columns can make for a more intimate and less urban environment, but the reduction in coverage from each unit will mean that more of them are required"* (DfT, 2007).

2.5.4 Pedestrian Planning and Design Guide, New Zealand (2008)

The document identifies and explains four concepts of improved pedestrian environment, namely, *living streets, pedestrian precincts, sharing the main street* and *shared zones* (NZ Transport Agency, 2008).

- *Living streets* emphasize that the streets be designed for living while maximizing the community interaction. They are to be so designed that the vehicles always remain aware of the pedestrians' presence. These shall utilise traffic-calming measures, hard and soft landscaping, places for social activities, children's play areas, seating, lighting, a good interface between street and housing as also the public art. The concept shall be relevant for roads that are not to serve through traffic predominantly.
- *Pedestrian precincts* are created by restricting traffic access or closing roads to traffic. These are most beneficial in the retail or mixed development areas that witness heavy pedestrian activity amidst motor traffic.

- *Sharing the main street* tends to manage certain arterial roads straddled by strips of retail, commercial and community activities but having conflicting traffic and pedestrian needs.
- *Shared zone* is a residential or retail street that prioritizes pedestrians while significantly discouraging the dominance of motorised vehicles. These are referred to as *home zones* in the United Kingdom and *woonerf* in the Netherlands. These are most suitable for streets and compact areas with a low demand for through traffic movement (NZ Transport Agency, 2008).

The document also identifies a variety of components and techniques that can be used to improve our networks for the benefit of pedestrians. *Traffic-reduction engineering techniques* include changing the priority at intersections by using Stop and Give Way signs; using a 'diverter' to prevent some through and/or turning movements at intersections; partially closing the street by using a kerb extension to block one direction of motor vehicle travel into or out of an intersection; closing the street to all vehicles by installing a physical barrier. *Traffic calming* covers a range of self-enforcing measures that slow traffic by making higher speeds feel uncomfortable to drivers. This is most appropriate in residential and retail areas. *Shared-use paths* offer path sharing for both the pedestrians and the cyclists, where the combined flow of pedestrian and cyclists is light.

2.5.5 Better Streets Plan, San Francisco (2010)

The Better Streets Plan provides a blueprint for the future of San Francisco's pedestrian environment. The Plan seeks to balance the needs of all street users, and reflects the understanding that the pedestrian environment is about much more than just transportation – that streets serve the whole multitude of social, recreational and ecological needs that must be considered when deciding on the most appropriate design. The document contains a wide range of guidelines relating to streetscape and pedestrian facilities. Major themes and ideas include *distinctive, unified streetscape design; space for public life; enhanced pedestrian safety; improved street ecology; universal design and accessibility; integrating pedestrians with transit; creative use of parking lanes; traffic calming to reduce speeding and enhance pedestrian safety; pedestrian-priority designs; and extensive greening* (SFPD, 2010).

2.6 Global Practices for Enhanced Walkability

As the negative environmental and social consequences of new mobility patterns become explicit, the cities across the world endeavour to improve liveability of their respective urban areas. Walkability, being pivotal to the liveability or sustainability agenda, is receiving increased attention globally in terms of policies and practices for absorption at segment level, area level and at comprehensive city level. While the European cities are a forerunner in this regard, American cities too have brought in policy changes to incorporate pedestrian spirits in their respective jurisdictions. The rest of the world too shows signs of change. These various interventions primarily pertain to the reduction of vehicle speeds, putting restrictions on the use of motorised transport, checking any vehicle–pedestrian collisions, providing adequate space protection and amenities to pedestrians along roads, ensuring safety in street crossing and people-oriented urban designs (CSE, 2009).

2.6.1 Traffic-calming measures

The term traffic calming is an English translation of the German *verkehrsberuhigung*. The traffic-calming movement began in Europe in the 1960s and spread steadily in North America after the late 1970s (Wheeler, 2013). Traffic calming covers a range of self-enforcing measures that reduce vehicle speeds and volumes on a particular roadway. The method is essentially a matter of limiting the length of unconstrained street sections so that speeds do not exceed target values. Traffic calming generally involves measures that slow traffic by making higher speeds feel uncomfortable to drivers. This means physically diverting a moving vehicle horizontally or vertically, sometimes accompanied by measures that have a psychological effect on drivers and encourage them to reduce their speed voluntarily (NZ Transport Agency, 2008). The various devices used in this context are discussed hereafter (Figure 2.13):

- *Speed humps* are perhaps the most common across many cities in the world. These are vertical deflection devices, 7–10 cm high and 3–4 m long, that reduce vehicle speeds to around 15 miles per hour without placing any restriction on traffic volumes. Sharper *speed bumps* reduce speed to about 5 miles per hour, but cause annoyance to the drivers. *Rumble strips* make noise when

driven over causing discomfort. *Speed tables* or *raised crosswalks* are raised sections of pavement much broader than speed humps.
- *Chicanes* are curb bulges or offset planters (usually 3) on alternate sides, forcing motorists to travel a zigzag path down the local streets.
- *Bulb-outs* or *chokers* are *curb extensions* into the street at intersections that narrow traffic lanes to control traffic and reduce pedestrian crossing distances.
- *Median islands* raised in the centre of the roadway reduce the lane width and provide pedestrians with a safe refuge in case of wide roadways that are difficult to traverse in a single traffic cycle.
- Small *traffic circles* at neighbourhood intersections as also *channelization islands* force traffic in a particular direction.
- *Colour and/ or textured pavements* make psychological impact on the drivers to slow down for being in the pedestrian priority zone.
- *Tighter corner radii* at the street corners force the drivers to reduce turning speeds.

Speed tables   Chicanes   Bulb-outs or chokers

Median island with a raised mid-block pedestrian crossing   Traffic circles   Color and/or textured pavements

Figure 2.13 Traffic-calming devices
[*Source*: https://en.wikipedia.org/wiki/Traffic_calming and NZ Transport Agency, 2008]

- The other traffic calming approaches focus on reducing the traffic volume rather than traffic speed. These use *diverters* to prevent some through and/or turning movements at intersections and *street closures* that close the street to all vehicles by installing a physical barrier. However, *diverters* have the disadvantage of diverting traffic onto other streets, which may then experience even worse problems (Wheeler, 2013).

The use of traffic calming measures in the European cities has increasingly facilitated the pedestrians, children and other non-motorized users to enjoy the neighbourhood streets as much as the motorized users. *"Physical constraints are created for vehicles utilizing landscaping and other structural measures with no delineation between footpath and roadway. This slows vehicles, reduces vehicle numbers and creates an 'environment of care' where motorized traffic would have a specific reason (trash removal vans, service vehicles, etc.) for travelling through the street. Environmental conditions and road safety improve to the benefit of residents, and streets become open spaces for walking, sitting, playing and talking"* (CSE, 2009).

Various neighbourhood-level movements, *woonerf* (living yard) in Netherlands and Germany, *home zones* in United Kingdom, *livable streets* in Britain, *shared zones*, etc., sought to improve the street environment through pedestrianisation. Traffic calming became an important tool to achieve the objective. A *woonerf* is the most developed form of traffic calming, imposes even more restrictions on car users with cars required to travel at walking speed near schools, offices and recreational opportunities. *Home zones* are primarily residential streets with limited traffic speed within which street activity including playing is treated as lawful and proactive attention is given to the parking issue. The current wave of traffic-calming devices in North America appears to encompass circles, humps and bulb-outs, which slow traffic without diversions. Circles in particular are used extensively by Portland, Seattle and Vancouver (Wheeler, 2013).

2.6.2   Other measures

Various cities are working towards invigorating their walking culture using severe measures and regulations, and trying to ensure strict enforcement through law (CSE, 2009).
- In Barcelona, walk trips were encouraged through combined strategies of mixed land use, low public transit fares and integrated

ticketing system; while the high rates of parking and other auto restrictive measures prohibited car use.
- European cities have made driver training institutes very expensive. Further, the drivers are expected to drive carefully and yield to pedestrians and cyclists even if they are jaywalking, ignoring traffic signals or behaving contrary to traffic regulations.
- Many of the Dutch and German cities have adopted the reduction of parking spaces in pedestrian areas. In order to discourage auto travel to the core of the cities, parking facilities are reserved to the core edges.
- Many American cities declared their downtown commercial districts as pedestrian zones thus giving priority to pedestrians while allowing access to vehicles only for servicing.
- Increased parking prices, parking permits for on-street non-metered parking and special limited parking meters in residential areas have proved effective for reigning in auto use.
- Arlington, Virginia, has adopted the concept of residential neighbourhoods with maximum facilities located within distances that are easily accessible on foot, by cycling and mass transit.
- An ordinance for better street policy has been passed in San Francisco to encourage walking through good street design and sound environmental planning. This ordinance requires all departments to work in co-ordination with each other regarding the design, planning and use of the public right of way.
- In Florida, the city government undertook road space reallocation as a traffic-calming measure. Several main street roads of Atlantic Boulevard in Del Ray Beach and West Palm Beach County were reduced from 4 to 2 lane and 4 to 3 lane.

2.7 Conclusion

It follows from literature that the built environment of neighbourhoods may become instrumental in enhancing or suppressing the pedestrian spirits. This illuminates the relevant professionals as regards their probable course of action in future to achieve the desired goals. The attempts in the various cities across the globe further strengthen our resolve to make our Indian cities more liveable and pedestrian friendly.

References

- Alfonzo, M., Boarnet, M.G., Day, K., Mcmillan, T., and Anderson, C.L. (2008). The relationship of neighbourhood built environment features and adult parents' walking. *Journal of Urban Design* 13(1): 29-51.
- Clifton, K.J., Livi Smith, A.D., and Rodriguez, D. (2007). The development and testing of an audit for the pedestrian environment. *Landscape and Urban Planning* 80(1-2): 95-110.
- CSE (2009). *Footfalls: Obstacle Course to Livable Cities.* Centre for Science and Environment, Delhi. <http://www.cseindia.org/userfiles/walkability_pdf.pdf>
- Department for Transport (DfT) (2007). *Manual for Streets.* Thomas Telford Publishing, London, UK.
- Ewing, R. (2000). *Pedestrian and Transit-Friendly Design: A Primer for Smart Growth.* EPA Smart Growth Network, ICMA, Washington, DC. <http://www.epa.gov/dced/pdf/ptfd_primer.pdf>
- Ewing, R., and Handy, S. (2009). Measuring the unmeasurable: Urban design qualities related to walkability, *Journal of Urban Design* 14(1): 65-84.
- Gallion, A.B., and Eisner, S. (eds.) (1984). *The Urban Pattern: City Planning and Design.* CBS Publishers, Delhi, pp 223-226.
- GDOT (2003). *Pedestrian and Streetscape Guide.* Georgia Department of Transportation. Otak, Inc.
- Horn, A. (2004). Reflections on the concept and conceptualization of the urban neighborhood in societies in transition: The case of Pretoria (South Africa). *Dela*, Vol. 21, pp. 329-340.
- Lynch, K. (1984). Good City Form. The MIT Press, England, pp. 400-402.
- MAoG (2005). *Pedestrian Policies and Design Guidelines.* Maricopa Association of Governments.
- Mehta, V. (2008). Walkable streets: Pedestrian behavior, perceptions and attitudes. *Journal of Urbanism: International Research on Placemaking and Urban Sustainability* 1(3): 217-245.

- NZ Transport Agency (2008). *Pedestrian Planning and Design Guide*. New Zealand.
- Parks, J.R., and Schofer, J.L. (2006). Characterizing neighbourhood pedestrian environments with secondary data. Transportation Research Part D: *Transport and Environment* 11(4): 250-263.
- SFPD (2010). *San Francisco Better Streets Plan – Policies and Guidelines for the Pedestrian Realm*. San Francisco Planning Department. <http://www.sfbetterstreets.org>
- Singhal, M., and Chahal, K.S. (2015). Role of built environment variables in enhancing walkability of neighbourhoods. *Journal of the Indian Institute of Architects* 80(4): 13-18.
- Talen, E. (2002). Pedestrian access as a measure of urban quality. *Planning Practice and Research* 17(3): 257-278.
- TfL (2004). *Making London a Walkable City – The Walking Plan for London*. Transport for London. <http://www.tfl.gov.uk>
- Tibbalds, F. (2005). *Making People-Friendly Towns: Improving the Public Environment in Towns and Cities*. Spon Press, London and New York.
- Wheeler, S. M. (2013). *Planning for sustainability: Creating livable, equitable and ecological communities*. Routledge, London and New York.
- Whittick, A. (ed.) (1974). *Encyclopedia of Urban Planning*. McGraw-Hill Book Company, USA. pp. 714-715.
- WSDT (1997). *Pedestrian Facilities Guidebook – Incorporating Pedestrians into Washington's Transportation System*. Washington State Department of Transportation.

3
Pedestrian Awakening in the Indian Cities

Pedestrians are in peril and are fast vanishing from the urban scene because of the perceptible threats and other factors. However the sustainable development practices at the global level are increasingly recognizing the importance of walkable environments because of their positive social, health and environmental implications. Consequently, various governments across the globe are attempting to make their cities and neighbourhoods more pedestrian friendly. Sustenance of the renewed spirits lies to a large extent in the legislative framework that dictates the built environment of our cities. It becomes pertinent that we explore the various government policies, rules and regulations regarding their likely impact on the pedestrian culture in the cities. In this context, this chapter brings forth the legislations at various levels of governance that could be instrumental in promoting the sustained pedestrian spirits in the context of Indian cities. The chapter also discusses the initiatives of a few organizations that have contributed for the enhancement of walkability of Indian cities. The following section is also discussed elsewhere (Singhal, 2018).

3.1 Exploring Pedestrian Concerns in the Existing Policy Framework and Legislation

The various policies and legislations in India that have important implications in dealing with urban transport are mostly administered by the central government. The Ministry of Urban Development is the nodal ministry for urban transport that handles strategic planning and policy formulation. Along with the Indian Roads Congress (IRC), this ministry is also responsible for laying down standards and norms for various components of urban transport (EPC, 2013). As per the Constitution of India, responsibility for urban development, and therefore, urban transport, rests with the state government (EPC, 2013). At the State level, urban development authorities and the department of transport handle significant part of the decisions. Local governments with their limited role in transport planning bear the responsibility of their maintenance (NTDPC, 2014).

The subsequent sections seek to explore the various policies and legislations that would impact significantly on the pedestrian-related issues in the city. It is pertinent to assess their effectiveness in safeguarding the pedestrian interests.

3.1.1 Policies for transport development

Urban transport in India has, in the past, received policy attention in an intermittent and often disjointed manner (NTDPC, 2014). This section explores the most recent policies that regulate traffic and transport in India from the pedestrian perspective.

National Urban Transport Policy (2014): The rapidly growing transport-related problems in the urban areas could adversely impact on the economic growth and quality of life. The Government of India, therefore, brought in the National Urban Transport Policy (NUTP) in April 2006 to bring about comprehensive improvements in urban transport services and infrastructure. NUTP 2006 was subsequently revised in 2014 based on a comprehensive review by Institute of Urban Transport India (IUT), a professional body promoted by MoUD, with the financial support of Shakti Foundation.

The policy clearly acknowledges the vulnerability of NMT modes in the current traffic scenario in Indian cities. The reasons cited for increased risks to the pedestrians and the cyclists are the shared right-of-way for motorized and non-motorized modes, encroachment of footpaths, badly designed pedestrian paths and cycle tracks, and lack of safe pedestrian crossing facilities at busy intersections. Urban sprawl too has added to the woes of the non-motorized modes. The risks involved and increased travel distances are understood to have led to the gradual disappearance of pedestrians and the cyclists from the urban scene. Key features of NUTP 2014 with respect to pedestrian concerns are hereafter brought forth:

- The policy proposes a paradigm shift in the urban transport approach with its three key strategies: 'Avoid, Shift and Improve', thereby meaning,

- to *avoid* increase in travel demand by reducing the number and length of trips,
  - to promote a *shift* from personal vehicles to other MRT and NMT modes, and
  - to *improve* the use of clean fuels and clean vehicle technology.
- The policy emphasizes on an equitable allocation of road space based on the people rather than the vehicles. Exclusive lanes and corridors are proposed for the PT and NMT modes.
- Pedestrian concerns are reflected in terms of segregated lanes, better pavement facilities and amenities such as shade-giving landscaping, provision of drinking water and resting stations to counter the adverse weather conditions. At the micro-level, the street design must provide for proper lighting while avoiding dead-ends or dreary, dark spaces. It also supports elements for universal accessibility such as adequate footpath widths, tactile plates on the pavement, anti-skid pavings, table-top road crossing facilities, signage supplemented with Braille and pictograms, lifts, etc.
- The policy acknowledges the need for an open debate with experts and the community for the design of these facilities to enable greater use by the potential beneficiaries.
- To ensure safety and enhanced use of NMT modes, the central government gives priority to the construction of cycle tracks and pedestrian paths in all cities under the National Urban Renewal Mission (NURM).
- The policy emphasizes that the fund allocation for major transport infrastructure should be linked to achieving targets for creating facilities for NMT. It suggests the creation of a separate budget head and a separate cell in the municipalities for the planning, design implementation and maintenance of such facilities.
- Because of environment friendliness of NMT modes, the policy seeks to encourage greater use of these by offering Central financial assistance. It offers monetary support for the construction of safe pedestrian crossings at busy intersections and high traffic corridors, as also the formulation and implementation of 'specific area plans in congested urban areas that propose appropriate mix

of various modes of transport including exclusive zones for non-motorized transit'.
- Parking is a major hindrance to the safe and smooth movement of non-motorized modes. Therefore, appropriate changes in bye-laws and legislation would be considered to free the public carriage way from parked vehicles in the residential areas while also making available adequate parking space for all residents/users of such buildings. The focus shall be on promoting parking as a demand management tool instead of increasing the parking supplies. The strategy would be to build parking for each neighbourhood development while avoiding parking for individual buildings. Standards can vary from zone to zone or city to sub-urban areas within the city and may be reviewed periodically and revised if necessary. Proposals for parking complexes would also be given priority under the NURM.
- The policy acknowledges the need for concerted efforts at all levels of governance to address the issues of sustainability in urban transport systems. It highlights the need for public awareness and cooperation in this regard. It seeks to launch intensive awareness campaigns so as to promote *'green travel habits'*.

The policy highlights the need to adopt green travel habits and encourages cities to develop relevant facilities but it does not clearly spell out the efforts the state and local administration must take in concrete terms. The policy therefore is suggestive, and does not seek to create any mandatory tasks. Further, walkability is considered mainly for higher hierarchy of roads or on routes to major traffic nodes.

Jawaharlal Nehru Urban Renewal Mission: Jawaharlal Nehru Urban Renewable Mission (JNNURM), a programme of the Union ministry of urban development for cities with more than a million population, aims to bring about integrated development of infrastructure services in selected cities, and offers the opportunity for their implementation. Under the JNNURM programme the cities are required to develop their respective city development plans (CDP) and identify the infrastructure projects that can be eligible for central and state assistance. The JNNURM has channelized a significant investment in transport systems for some of India's largest cities (NTDPC, 2014). In most cases, pedestrian ways become implicit in the overall road infrastructure planning for the city.

National Transport Development Policy Committee (2010): In 2010, the Government of India constituted National Transport Development Policy Committee to formulate a long-term transport policy for the country. The Committee stressed the need to address the mobility needs of people in the urban areas rather than facilitation of higher vehicle speeds. It emphasized on prioritizing non-motorized transport, public transport and para-transit, and personal vehicles in that order in addressing the mobility needs. The Committee insists the need for citywide facilities for the non-motorized transport, i.e. safe routes and the accompanying facilities such as parking booths, drinking water kiosks and street furniture. The NTDPC recommends that all cities should be bound, through law, to provide pedestrian facilities and ensure their maintenance within a period of 10 years (NTDPC, 2014).

3.1.2 Acts and rules pertaining to the pedestrians

Several provisions exist in the various legislations that have a direct or an implied bearing on the pedestrians. There is no legislation at present that covers the requirements of urban transport comprehensively.

- The Indian Penal Code, 1860 through Section 279 prohibits rash driving or riding on a public way and through Section 283 prohibits danger or obstruction in public way or line of navigation making either of these a punishable offence. The Section 279, 304A, 336, 337 and 338 are designed to prevent any rash and negligent acts that may endanger human life or the personal safety of others, thereby including the pedestrians as well (EPC, 2013; CSE, 2009). As per Section 283 of the IPC, vending shall be an obstruction in a public space (CSE, 2009).
- Motor Vehicles Act, 1988 puts restrictions on the granting of learners licenses for certain vehicles indirectly protecting the road users.
- Rules of the Road Regulations, 1989 delineates the responsibilities of motorists with respect to the pedestrians. Rule 8 cautions the drivers of motor vehicles at road junctions and pedestrian crossings to slow down for ensuring safety of persons. Rule 11 upholds the pedestrian right-of-way at uncontrolled pedestrian crossings and prohibits driving on such foot paths and cycle tracks. Rule 15 prohibits parking of the motor vehicle on a

footpath or near a traffic light or pedestrian crossing so as not to cause danger, obstruction or undue inconvenience to other road users.
- The National Road Safety and Traffic Management Board Bill, 2010 mandates the Board, through Article 3(h), to provide for the special requirements of women, children, senior citizens, disabled persons and pedestrians through road safety and traffic management measures in relation to the national highways and mechanically propelled vehicles.
- It is observed that the legislations are unambiguous as regards the responsibilities of the motorists making the offenders liable to punishment; however they recognize the pedestrians in a lukewarm and often implied manner (Bhardwaj, 2010).

3.1.3 Norms and standards for pedestrian design

For a long time, urban roads in India have remained guided by the Codes of Practice issued by the Indian Roads Congress (IRC) as early as 1970s and 1980s. These codes and eventually the traditional traffic engineering practice have remained vehicle-centric. Recognizing the changed transport scenario, these codes have been reviewed separately by IRC and Ministry of Urban Development (MoUD), Government of India. The IRC's first revision of the guidelines for pedestrian facilities emphasizes on the need to design streets for all users and activities (IRC, 2012). The MoUD got prepared the 'Code of Practice' for various urban road components through the Institute of Urban Transport (IUT) in association with the Transport Research and Injury Prevention Programme (TRIPP), IIT, Delhi. These guidelines give priority to the requirements of pedestrians, non-motorized modes and the public transport over private transport modes in urban areas. The codes also recognize the requirements of inclusive mobility in the proposed design standards (MoUD, 2013). In the absence of any city- or state-specific street guidelines, the recommendations of IRC or MoUD may guide any street design practices in the country (EPC, 2013). The following section seeks to extract pedestrian-related guidelines and standards recommended for the Indian cities. The IRC document being more explicit and focused is the major reference.

The pedestrian design must provide for integrated and barrier-free pedestrian facilities to ensure inclusive mobility and universal accessibility. The quality of the footpath facility is determined based on nine parameters: *footpath width, surface, obstruction, encroachment, potential of vehicular conflict, continuity, safety and security, comfort and walk environment.* The former six pertain to the physical characteristics and the latter three are the user factors.

1. Footpath width

Footpaths have three distinct zones that serve separate purposes: *Pedestrian zone* provides continuous unobstructed space for walking; *frontage zone* provides a buffer between street-side activities and the pedestrian zone; and *furniture zone* provides space for landscaping, furniture, lights, bus stops, signs and private property access ramps (Figure 3.1).

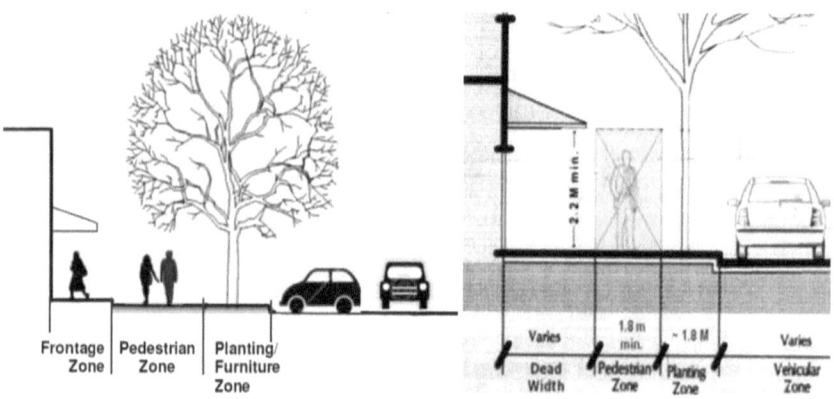

Figure 3.1 Three distinct footpath zones [*Source*: UTTIPEC, 2010 and IRC, 2012]

The footpath width is governed by the right-of-way, desired level of service, expected pedestrian traffic and adjacent land use. A minimum of 1.8 m clear and unobstructed pathway width shall be ensured in each direction for roads with right-of-way of 10.0 m and above. This allows two wheelchair users to pass each other comfortably. The minimum acceptable value would be 1.5 m for roads narrower than 10 m or light pedestrian traffic, giving enough space to a wheelchair user and a walker to pass each other. Level of service B is an acceptable standard ensuring reasonable pedestrian facilities for pleasant and comfortable walking, though under resource constraint, level of service C may decide the width of footpath (Table 3.1). Desired clear minimum width is 1.8 m in residential/ mixed use areas and 2.5 m in the commercial areas. In addition, a dead width of 0.5 m may be added where footpaths adjoin buildings or fences.

Table 3.1 Level of Service (LOS) criteria for width of sidewalk

Width of sidewalk (meters)	Design flow in number of persons per hour			
	In both directions		All in one direction	
	LOS B	LOS C	LOS B	LOS C
1.8	1350	1890	2025	2835
2.0	1800	2520	2700	3780
2.5	2250	3150	3375	4725
3.0	2700	3780	4050	5670
3.5	3150	4410	4725	6615
4.0	3600	5040	5400	7560

[*Source*: IRC, 2012]

2. Footpath surface

Footpaths should have firm and evenly paved walking surfaces to prevent falling and puddle forming. All walking surfaces should be non-skid or matt finish. Any break in the surface such as drainage channels or gratings should not be greater than 12 mm and should be aligned perpendicular to the direction of movement to prevent walking sticks and wheels getting caught in the gaps. Service covers to manholes and inspection chambers should not be positioned on footpaths, particularly at dished crossings. Crossfalls shall be provided, only when absolutely necessary for drainage purposes, to a maximum slope of 1:50.

3. Kerb height and radius

The height of a pavement (including kerb, walking surface, top-of-paving) shall not exceed 150 mm above the road level (Figure 3.2). Medians should be maximum 250 mm high or be replaced by crash barriers. Corner kerb radius shall be small as it increases pedestrian safety through reduced crossing distances and vehicle speeds as also increased pedestrian visibility for the drivers while turning. Maximum corner kerb radius of 12 m may be reduced to 6 m in residential areas. This slows down the turning buses, trucks, etc. Provision of a corner mountable kerb for turning of emergency vehicles shall however be made. The left turning slip roads at the road junctions are undesirable for pedestrian safety and should be avoided at intersections up to 30 m right-of-way.

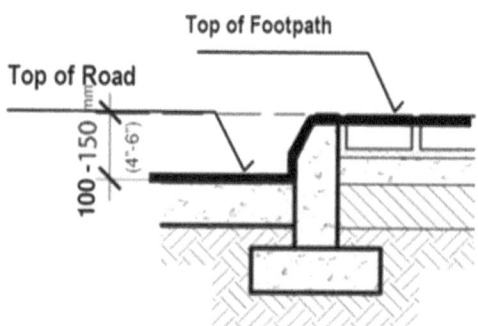

Figure 3.2 Kerb height [*Source*: IRC, 2012]

4. Accessibility features

Kerb ramps: Kerb ramps at main crossing points facilitate persons using prams or wheel chairs. These should be provided at the street intersection but located away from corners and on both street sides (Figure 3.3). Standard kerb ramps are cut into the footpath at a gradient not steeper than 1:12 with flared sides of maximum 1:10 gradient thus providing transition in three directions. Width of the kerb ramp should not be less than 1.2 meters (Figure 3.4). Tactile warning strips are to be provided on the kerbside edge of slope. Kerb ramps should have tactile pavers.

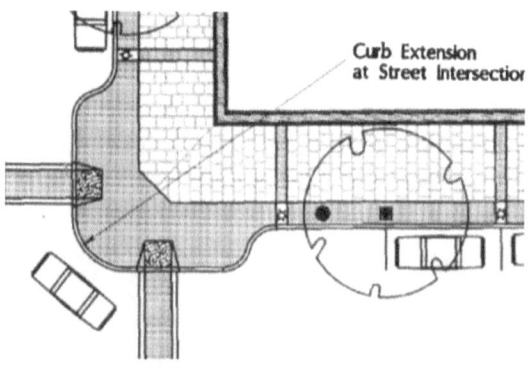

Figure 3.3 Location of kerb ramps at street intersection [*Source*: UTTIPEC, 2010]

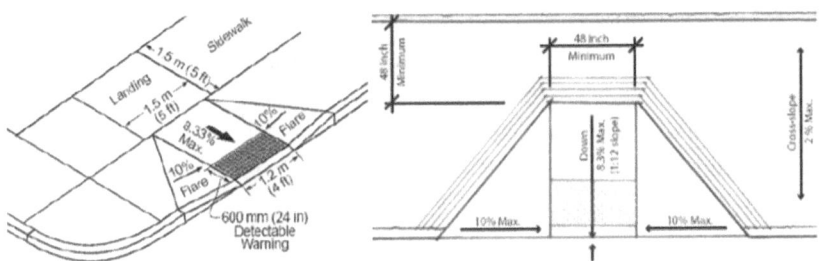

Figure 3.4 Views of kerb ramp cut into the pavement [*Source*: IRC, 2012 and UTTIPEC, 2010]

Tactile paving: For the purpose of guiding and warning those with vision impairment, tactile pavers should be used along the path of travel. These should utilize consistent textures which are different from the rest of the footway and do not confuse persons with vision impairments. Guide blocks have straight continuous lines and indicate the correct path/route to follow leading to building entrances, an amenity, bus stop, etc. Warning blocks are dotted or blistered and provide warning signal to screen-off obstacles, drop-offs or other hazards, to discourage movement in an incorrect direction and to give warning of a corner or junction (Figure 3.5).

Figure 3.5 Guide blocks and warning blocks forming guiding path to the building
[*Source*: IRC, 2012]

Tactile paving should be placed 300 mm at the beginning and end of the ramps, stairs and entrances to any door. A distance of 600–800 mm shall be maintained from the edge of footpath or boundary wall or any other obstruction. A height of about 5 mm for the raised part of the surface is sufficient for almost all persons with vision impairment to detect, without causing too much discomfort for other pedestrians. Tactile paving must be maintained to ensure that the profile does not erode away. Vitrified non-glazed tactile pavers are preferable. Tactile tiles should have a colour, preferably canary yellow, which contrasts with the surrounding surface. Tactile paving should be provided in the line of travel avoiding obstructions such as manholes/ tree guards/ lamp posts, etc.

Auditory signal: Audible crossing signals (pelican crossings) help everyone, as well as being essential for persons with vision impairments. Pedestrian traffic lights should be provided with clearly audible signals to facilitate safe and independent crossing of pedestrians with low vision and vision impairment. Acoustic devices should be installed on a pole at the point of origin of crossing and not at the point of destination.

5. Footpath continuity and street elements

The continuity of footpath in the public right-of-way should be maintained incorporating various obstructions. Where required to enable the access to private properties, vehicle ramps should be provided in the landscaping strip but not in the area of pedestrian through movement. Ending the footpath with abrupt curbs or lowering the entire footpath to the level of the carriageway is unacceptable as property entrances may become waterlogged. Bus stops should be located in a way that allows for a minimum 1.8 m of walking space behind the shelter. Bus bays are to be avoided. Instead, the bus shelter should be brought forward to the bus' linear line of travel to improve its usability. Parking is a flexible street element that should only be provided where there is sufficient space in the right-of-way after adequate provisions have been made for pedestrian facilities. Parking bays should be avoided at intersections, bus stops, midblock crossings, or locations with unavoidable changes in the right-of-way that would compromise the width of the footpath. The material for the parking areas should be different from that of the carriage way to help define where parking is permitted and to prevent high-speed driving through parking bays.

6. Street furniture and amenities

Street furniture provides people places to sit, rest and interact with each other. Street furniture also includes services-related infrastructure such as trash cans, street vending, kiosks, toilets and signage. Furniture and amenities should be located where they are likely to be used and where these do not obstruct the pedestrian movement. Bulb-outs in parking lanes and street vending islands in shared streets are great places to install furniture. Similarly, a landscaping strip can be broken with street furniture on hardscaped spaces.

7. Multi-functional zone

Multifunctional planting zones with native street trees and plantation are essential on every street to provide shade and climatic comfort. Planting zones can also function as natural storm water catchments and filtration systems, aiding in ground water recharge, preventing seasonal flooding and reducing the pressure on piped storm water infrastructure. Multi-functional zones on a street may accommodate any or all such functions as tree planting, planting for storm water management, auto-rickshaw stands, cycle-rickshaw stands, hawker zones, car parking, street furniture, street lights/ pedestrian lights, bus stops, traffic police booths, fire hydrants, junction boxes, etc. (Figure 3.6). Multi-functional zones on a street should be a minimum of 1.8 m wide, and may locate multiple functions. Provision of these is most critical otherwise the uses/components of streets would encroach upon pedestrian, NMV or carriageway space. Common utility ducts and duct banks should not be located under the multi-functional zones as there may be interference due to trees.

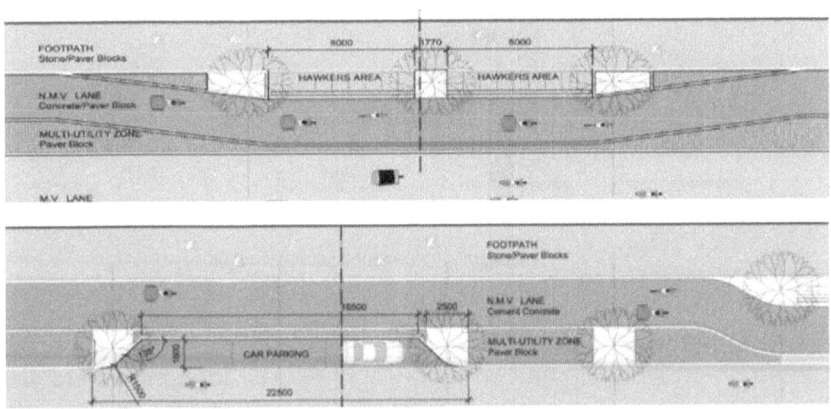

Figure 3.6 Multifunctional zone on a street [*Source*: UTTIPEC, 2010 and IRC, 2012]

8. Lighting

Lighting needs of pedestrians are different from those of vehicular traffic and therefore need to be designed and integrated within the overall lighting strategy for the street. The placement of street lighting should be coordinated with other street elements so that trees or advertisement hoardings do not impede proper illumination (Figure 3.7). For footpaths, white lighting at 25–40 lux is recommended. For pedestrian crossing, higher lighting level of 80 lux using special light poles is recommended. Height of light pole and luminaire type are a function of street width. 30 m or narrower streets like local access lanes, alleys and pedestrian pathways can be adequately illuminated with low-mast lighting fixtures (3–5 m tall) alone. For wide streets with high pedestrian/commercial activity, mid-mast lighting (10–12 m tall) may be combined with pedestrian scale lighting to create additional security and comfort. Lighting must be provided at an interval of 20–30 m and should focus on pedestrian lanes.

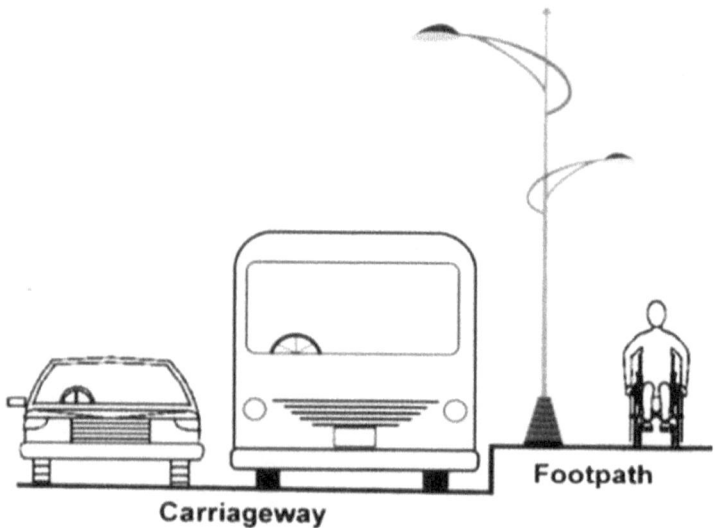

Figure 3.7 Lighting on the footpath [Source: IRC, 2012]

9. Pedestrian crossings and refuge islands

Pedestrian crossings, frequently required near the intersections as also at mid-block levels, may be at-grade or grade separated. However, the at-grade pedestrian crossings are of more frequent occurrence as they offer the shortest possible route for the pedestrians to cross the road. At-grade pedestrian crossings should be minimum 3.0 m wide and should provide for universal accessibility features and street directional signage. Formal mid-block pedestrian crossings should be provided at regular intervals with spacing ranging from 80 to 250 meters in residential and 80 to 150 meters in commercial/mixed use areas. These need to be coordinated with entry points of complexes, bus/train stops, public facilities, etc. To ensure safety, formal crossings should be signalized or should be constructed as Tabletop crossings with ramps for vehicles. Raised or Tabletop pedestrian crossings tend to emphasize the pedestrian presence on the road and reduce vehicle speeds. Kerb extensions at the intersection and at mid-block provide better visibility for the motorists and pedestrians especially when the street has kerbside parking facility (Figure 3.8).

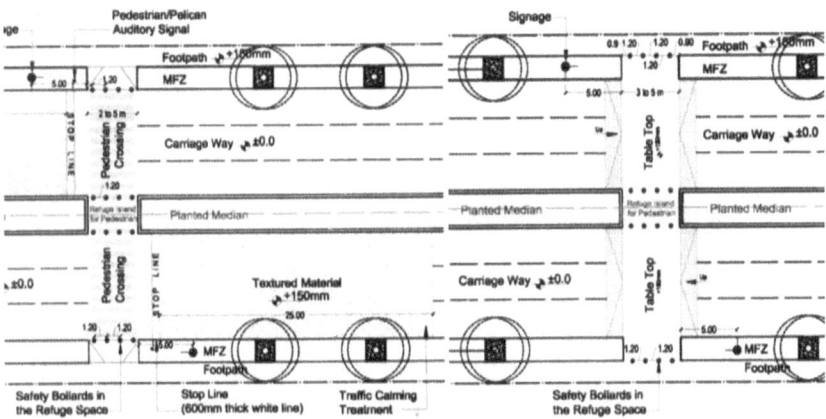

Figure 3.8 At-grade pedestrian crossings [*Source*: UTTIPEC, 2010 and IRC, 2012]

In case of multiple lanes, mid-block refuge island provides a safe haven for the pedestrians since it is extremely difficult to cross the entire carriageway width in a single shot. The pedestrian refuge enables the pedestrian to deal with traffic in a single direction only at one point of time. The refuge should be the same width as the pedestrian crossing and the depth should not be less than 2 m, enough to park a wheelchair. Safety bollards in the refuge space shall prevent U-turning of vehicles (Figure 3.9).

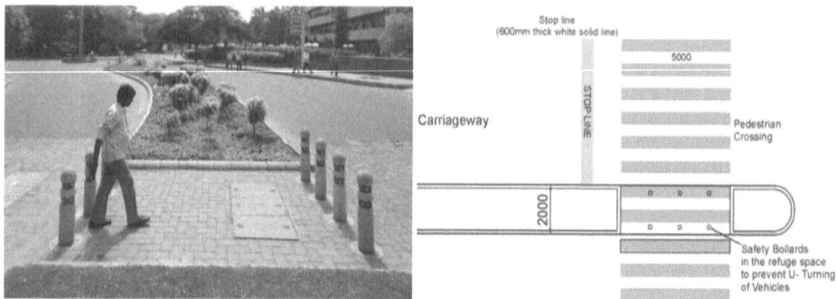

Figure 3.9 Typical pedestrian refuge at median [*Source*: UTTIPEC, 2010 and IRC, 2012]

3.2 Initiatives at Enhancing Walkability in Indian Cities

There are many organizations, international and local, currently working on and/or planning on improving walkability in India. Some of these are discussed in the subsequent paragraphs.

3.2.1 The Clean Air Initiative for Asian Cities (2001)

Established in 2001, the Clean Air Initiative for Asian Cities (CAI-Asia) is part of a global initiative that promotes better air quality and liveable cities. CAI-Asia with support and collaboration from various partners has been promoting the improvement of walkability and pedestrian facilities in many Asian cities. In India, CAI-Asia worked with the Shakti Foundation and completed a survey on walkability in selected Indian cities in 2010. After the walkability survey in six Indian cities of Bhubaneswar, Chennai, Indore, Pune, Rajkot and Surat, they held dialogues with the city government officials and other stakeholders to seek commitment for improving walkability and pedestrian facilities. Discussions were also held with other city governments like Hyderabad, Delhi and Chandigarh to see how challenges and further actions can be pursued. Some of the cities viz. Bhubaneswar, Chennai, Hyderabad expressed to improve the conditions by creating pedestrian only areas, capacity building for city engineers on complete street design concepts, etc. (CAI-Asia and SSEF, 2012).

3.2.2 Street Design Guidelines by UTTIPEC (2010)

Unified Traffic and Transportation Infrastructure, Planning and Engineering Centre (UTTIPEC) of DDA, New Delhi, put together the 'Street Design Guidelines' in 2010. Based on best practices available around the world, these set of guidelines were tailored to the ground realities in India. The UTTIPEC propagates that streets are valuable public spaces as well as movement corridors. Design of streets is a function of the street hierarchy and adjacent land uses. Design templates are provided that can be used to retrofit existing roads and also for new roads (Figure 3.10). The document offers a pedestrian design toolkit in terms of a set of 10 non-negotiable street design components as also additional guidelines for world class streets. Various mandatory components are components of the pedestrian-only zone (including kerb radii and slip roads), frontage zone or "dead width", universal accessibility features/ barrier-free design, multi-functional zone with planting for storm water management, bicycle and non-motorized transport (NMT) infrastructure, crossings, medians, refuge islands, street lighting, urban utilities, and public amenities (toilets, bus stops, dustbins), hawker zones, signage. Additional requirements mean traffic-calming measures, material selection, public art, street furniture and educative signage, BRT systems; bus and HOV lanes (UTTIPEC, 2010).

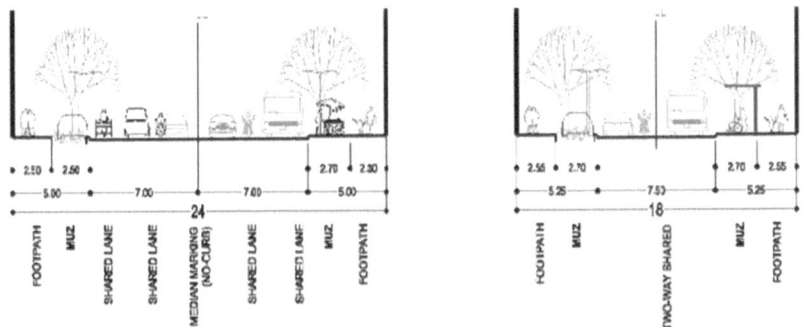

Figure 3.10 Templates for 24 m and 18 m roads with mixed-use zones [*Source*: UTTIPEC, 2010]

3.2.3 Better Streets, Better Cities: A Guide to Street Design in Urban India by ITDP and EPC (2011)

Institute for Transportation and Development Policy (ITDP) and Environmental Planning Collaborative (EPC) offer a guide for street design in India that attempts to articulate the concept of 'equitable allocation of road space', one of the key principles outlined in the NUTP. The guide provides a framework for understanding various elements of street design and a toolkit for well-designed streets. The document first identifies 16 elements that make up a street; and then presents principles that govern their placement and design, and offers photos of good and bad practices as also various design options. The document observes that the problem of Indian streets is that they are designed from the centreline outwards, prioritizing the vehicles while ignoring the rest. Consequently, pedestrians, trees, utilities, street vending and social activities often jostle for the insufficient leftover space.

The manual emphasizes the need to design complete streets that provide space for all users. Increasing the efficiency of streets rather than widening them can solve mobility problems. A complete street can take on a variety of forms, depending on factors such as the available right-of-way, traffic volumes, street-side activities, and adjacent land uses.

All streets that aim to maximize mobility also need separate slow zones for liveability for people to walk, talk and interact, for doing business, for children to play. In general, smaller right-of-ways can function as slow shared spaces used by both pedestrians and vehicles. Street vending and social activities can also take place in the shared space. A narrow driving lane and other traffic calming elements help keep vehicle speeds low, so that vehicle movement remains compatible with the other uses. A larger street can cater to walking and stationary activities as well as through movement, but it often makes sense to differentiate the slow, shared zone from the mobility zone to ensure comfort and safety for pedestrians and stationary users (Kost and Nohn, 2011).

The document provides a collection of street templates for a series of typical road widths to show how the various elements can be combined to provide varying degrees of liveability and mobility. The templates are shown in order of increasing street widths: 6, 7.5, 9, 12, 18, 24, 30, 36 and 42 m. A few of these are shown in Figures 3.11, 3.12 and 3.13. BRT templates too are provided for street widths ranging from 18 to 42 m.

3.2.4 The Centre for Science and Environment

The Centre for Science and Environment (CSE) is a public interest research and advocacy organization based in New Delhi. The Centre researches into, lobbies for and communicates the urgency of development that is both sustainable and equitable. It conducts various programs and conferences on mobility focused on non-motorized transport and advocates for automobile-independent cities (CAI-Asia and SSEF, 2012). The Right to Clean Air team at CSE conducted a random survey in selected locations in Delhi to assess the status of pedestrian walkways. The purpose was to identify the key barriers that undermine the quality of the pedestrian ways and understand the walking experience. Locales were selected to represent residential and commercial land-use classes and also low-income neighbourhoods. The team audited the walking infrastructure based on a range of criteria related to engineering design, overall environment of the walkways, quality of crosswalks and exposure to traffic. Pedestrian perception survey was also carried out to assess how pedestrians feel about the walking condition (CSE, 2011).

3.3 Conclusion

It becomes evident that the most recent policies and guidelines in India are exhibiting enough consideration for the pedestrians in a direct or an implied manner. However, the absence of any specific instructions towards the implementation of various provisions makes most of these ineffective or redundant. In this context, the walk-related policies and initiatives in the various cities across the globe build up a strong support for similar initiatives in Indian cities while also offering guidance towards actual implementation.

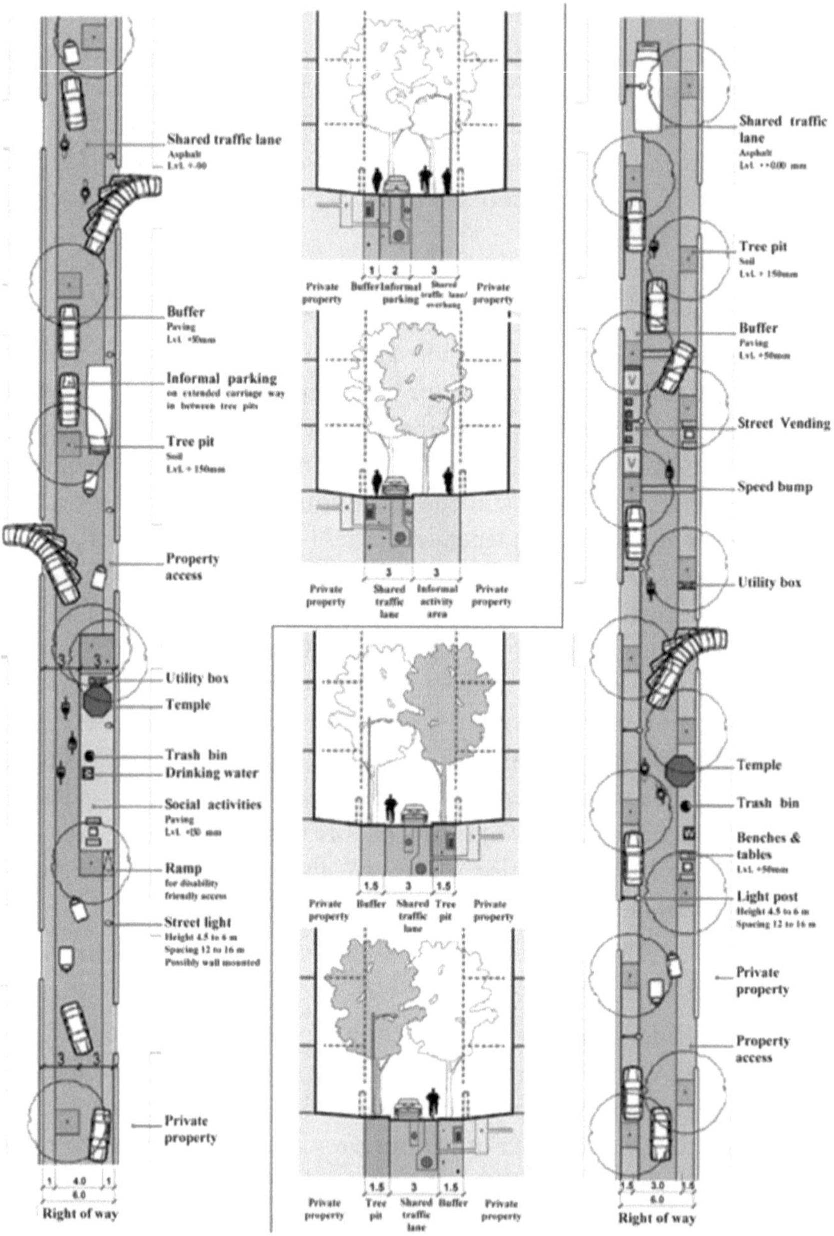

Option 1 Option 2

Figure 3.11 Templates for 6 m wide streets (with shared spaces) [*Source*: ITDP, 2011]

Pedestrian Awakening in the Indian Cities 61

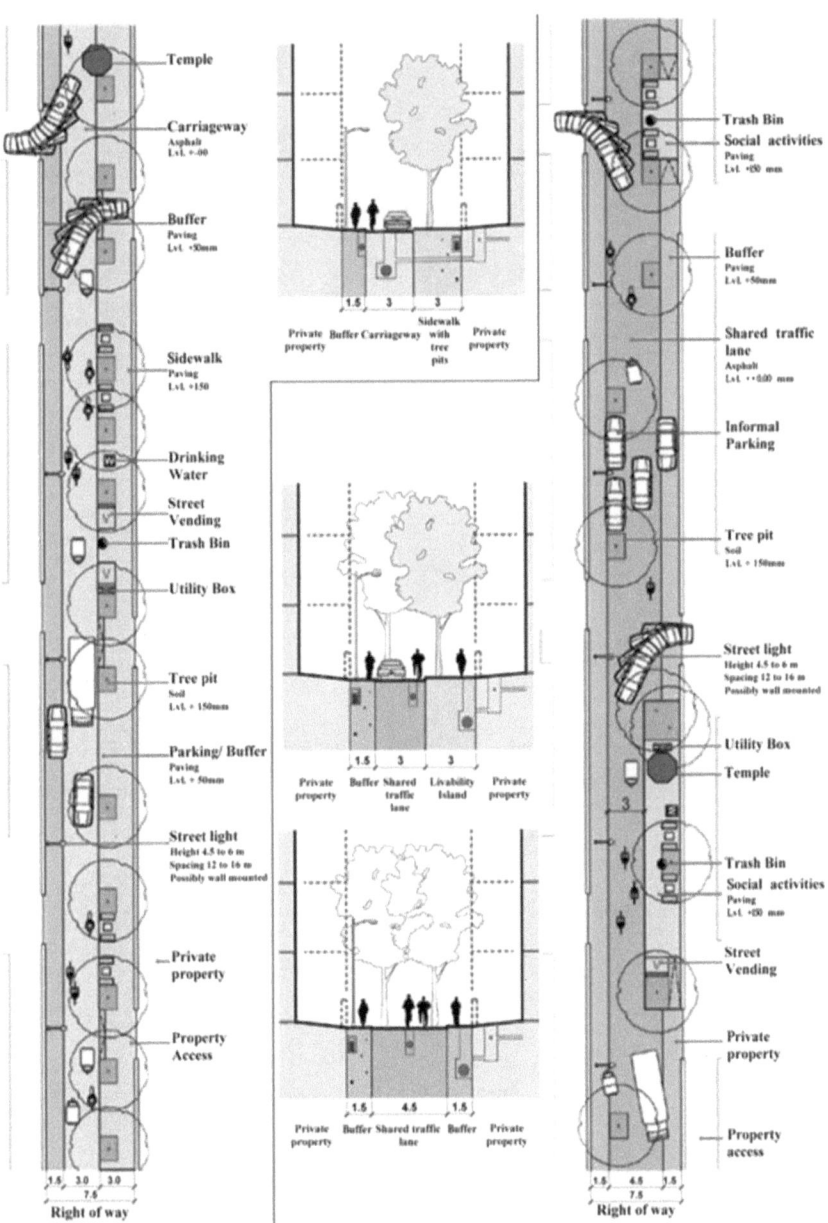

Street with footpaths   Street with shared spaces

Figure 3.12 Templates for 7.5 m wide streets [*Source*: ITDP, 2011]

62 Towards Pedestrian-Friendly Neighbourhoods

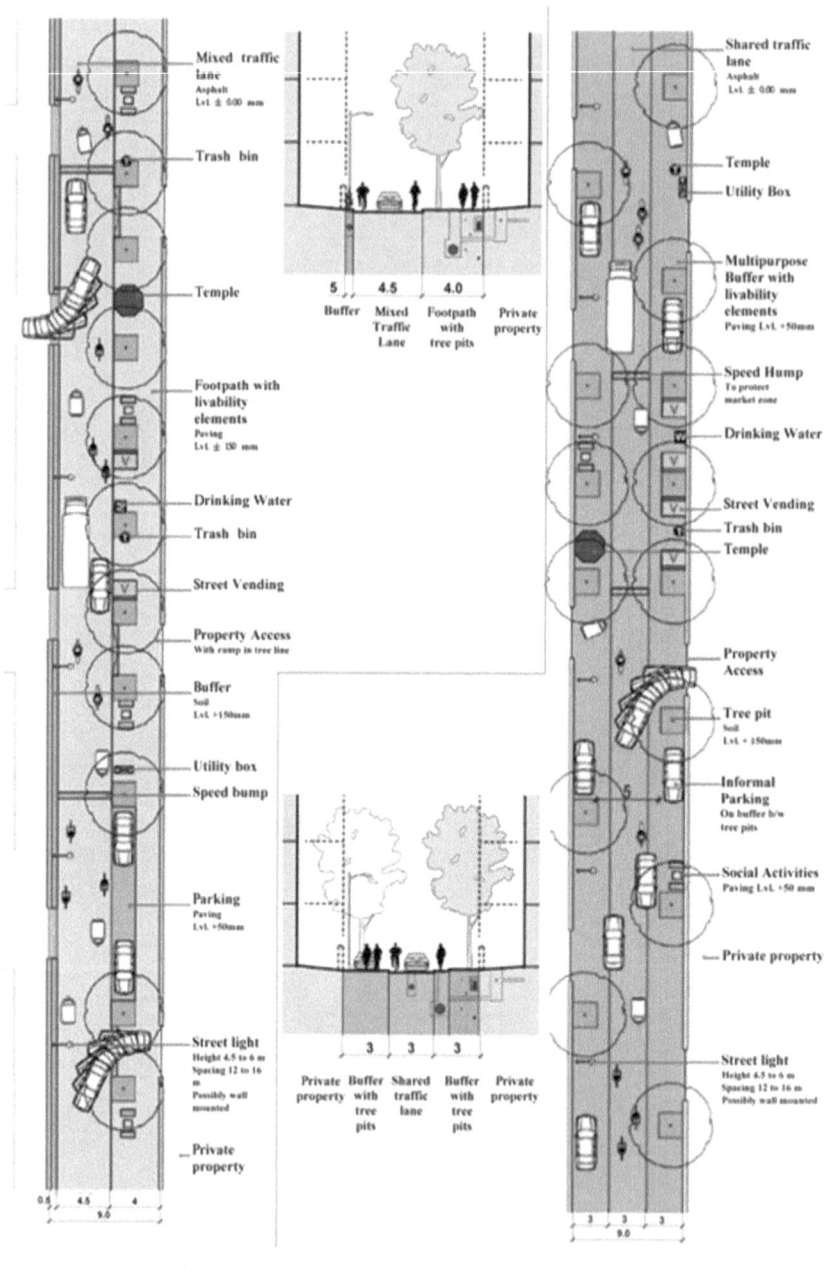

Figure 3.13 Templates for 9 m wide streets [Source: ITDP, 2011]

References

- Bhardwaj, P. (2010). *The Pedestrian and the Road.* Working Paper Series. Centre for Public Policy Research, Kerala. <http://www.cppr.in>
- CAI-Asia and SSEF (2012). *Improving Footpaths in Indian Cities through Walkability Surveys and Tighter Policies.* Clean Air Initiative for Asian Cities (CAI-Asia) Center and Shakti Sustainable Energy Foundation. Pasig City, Philippines.
- CSE (2009). *Footfalls: Obstacle Course to Livable Cities.* Centre for Science and Environment, Delhi. <http://www.cseindia.org/userfiles/walkability_pdf.pdf>
- EPC (2013). *Sustainable Urban Transport Principles and Implementation Guidelines for Indian Cities.* Environmental Planning Collaborative, Ahmedabad, India.
- IRC (1989). *Guidelines for Pedestrian Facilities.* Indian Roads Congress. IRC: 103-1988.
- IRC (2012). *Guidelines for Pedestrian Facilities (First Revision).* Indian Roads Congress. IRC: 103-2012.
- Kost, C., and Nohn, M. (2011). *Better Streets, Better Cities – A Guide to Street Design in Urban India.* Institute for Transportation and Development Policy (ITDP) and Environmental Planning Collaborative (EPC). <http://www.itdp.org/betterstreets>
- Singhal, M. (2018). *Walkability and Legislation: How Supportive is the Legislative Framework as regards Pedestrian Concerns in the Indian Cities?* In the proceedings of the 6th Annual International Conference on "Architecture and Civil Engineering (ACE-2018)" organized by Global Science and Technology Forum (GSTF) from 14th to 15th May 2018 in Singapore, pp. 212-218.
- MoUD (2006). *National Urban Transport Policy.* Ministry of Urban Development, Government of India, New Delhi.
- MoUD (2013). *Code of Practice for Design of Urban Roads.* Prepared by the Transportation Research and Injury Prevention Programme (TRIPP) for the Institute of Urban Transport (IUT), Ministry of Urban Development, Government of India.

- NTDPC (2014). *India Transport Report: Moving India to 2032*. National Transport Development Policy Committee. Published on behalf of Planning Commission, GOI. Routledge - Taylor and Francis Group, New Delhi.
- UTTIPEC (2010). *Street Design Guidelines*. Unified Traffic and Transportation Infrastructure (Planning and Engineering) Centre, DDA, New Delhi. <http://uttipec.nic.in/writereaddata/linkimages/7554441800.pdf>

4
Walk Scenario in the Neighbourhoods of Amritsar City: A Case Study

By ameliorating our neighbourhood built environments, we may expect an enhanced pedestrian culture in the Indian cities. As the first step, the neighbourhoods of Indian cities need to be explored to develop understanding of the prevalent walk scenario. In this context, the city of Amritsar is identified as the prototype of numerous metropolitan cities of India. A national level survey of 30 Indian cities (MoUD, 2008) highlights the poor walkability scenario along the major road network in Amritsar city (Chapter 1, Table 1.1). Expecting a similar scenario in its neighbourhoods as well, the built environments of the selected neighbourhoods are investigated utilising the adapted version of the Pedestrian Environment Data Scan (PEDS) Audit Tool. Simultaneously, the residents' feedback is sought as regards perception of their immediate environments from pedestrian perspective. Residents' expectations and preferences are explored so as to predict and understand their responsiveness to any future changes. Some of the following sections are differently discussed elsewhere (Singhal, 2015a, 2015b and 2015c).

4.1 Amritsar City: An Overview of Traffic and Pedestrian Scenario

Amritsar, literally meaning 'pool of nectar', is the religious and spiritual capital of Punjab and is identified by the Golden Temple, the most revered Sikh shrine in the world. The epic stories of the Golden Temple and Jallianwala Bagh have given this dynamic and striking city a unique place in the history of the country. The history of Amritsar is more than 400 years old and is intricately intertwined with the birth of Sikh religion. With its rich historical past, the city today emerges as a mosaic of various time periods it struggled through that bear an indelible imprint on the cityscape.

As per 2011 census, Amritsar has a population of 12,72,044 and is the second largest metropolitan city of Punjab. It ranked 33rd in the list of 35 metropolitan cities as per census 2001 and 274th in the world's list of 1000 largest urban settlements (PMIDC, 2012). The city, spread over an area of 139 sq. km, has gross developed area density of 125 persons per hectare.

4.1.1 Road traffic scenario and the pedestrian apathy

As per the Comprehensive Mobility Plan for Amritsar, the total number of registered vehicles in the city has been increasing at an average rate of 6.14 percent per year (PMIDC, 2012). However the road capacities have not got enhanced accordingly. The right-of-way (ROW) of the city roads ranges between 10 m to 60 m. While 71 percent of the road length has less than 30 m ROW, 60 percent of the road length has less than 15 m carriageway width; 40 percent of the roads have undivided carriageway; 93 percent of roads have no service roads. On-street parking is predominant (over 63 percent of road length) resulting in capacity reduction. This has led to reduction of speeds on roads. Average speed ranges from 11 to 40 kmph on arterial roads and 8 to 30 kmph on sub-arterial roads. Ever-increasing traffic congestion increases the vulnerability of population in terms of traffic hazards, high levels of noise, disturbing vibrations and air pollution.

Walking, in Amritsar, is an important mode of travel that accounts for 26.75 percent of all trips (Table 4.1). The per capita rate of travel trips works out to be 1.22 including walk trips and 0.88 excluding walk trips. The average trip length of walk trips works out to be 1.65 km. Walk trips up to 1 km in length accounted for a large share of 77 percent of all the walk trips. Trips longer than 2 km accounted for 6.2 percent of all walk trips. However the city offers formidable walking conditions. Pedestrian facilities are generally poor or absent. 87 percent of road length lacks footpaths. 59 percent road length lacks signage. 37 percent road length has no markings (PMIDC, 2012).

Table 4.1 Modal share in Amritsar

Transport mode		Percent share
Private modes	Two wheeler	25.9
	Cars	6.63
Public mass transport modes	Standard buses	1.9
	Mini bus	2.74
Intermediate public transport	Auto rickshaw	22.03
	Taxi	0.09
Non-motorised modes	Cycle	11.15
	Cycle rickshaw	2.53
	Walk	26.75

[*Source*: PMIDC, 2012]

In 2008, the Union Ministry of Urban Development, Government of India, undertook a national level survey for the purpose of formulating traffic and transportation-related policies and strategies in the urban areas of India (MoUD, 2008). A total of 30 cities of varied sizes were identified for the purpose. In addition to several important aspects of traffic and transportation, walkability too was studied through various surveys such as household interview surveys, pedestrian opinion surveys, road network inventory, etc. Various parameters such as walk trips, trip lengths and walkability index were considered in relation to the size of the cities. Comparison with other cities of the country indicates that though the share of walk trips in Amritsar city is higher than the national average, walkability conditions are much more formidable (Table 1.1 of Chapter 1, Figures 4.1 and 4.2).

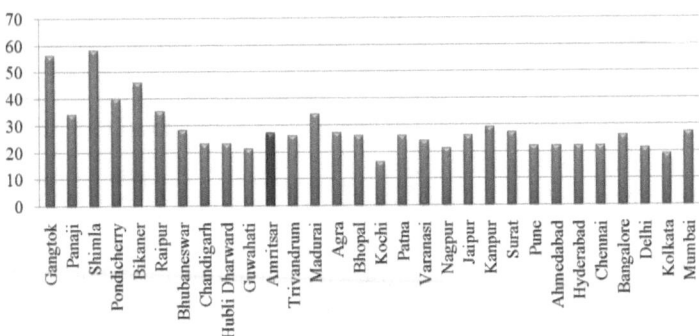

Figure 4.1 Share of walk trips (percent) for the selected cities [*Source*: MoUD, 2008]

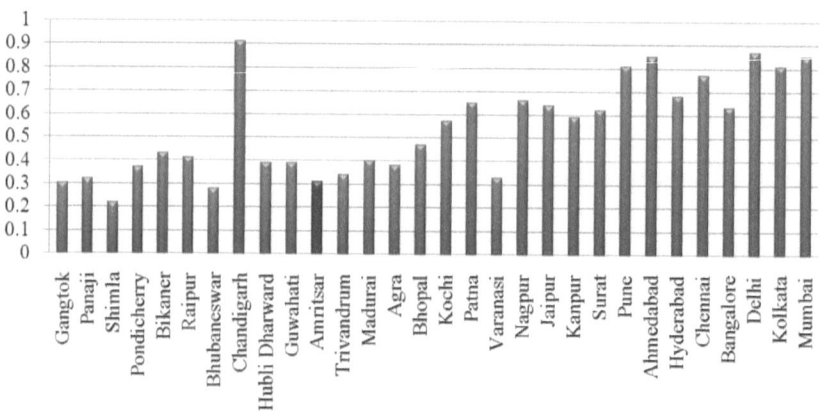

Figure 4.2 Walkability Index for the selected cities [*Source*: MoUD, 2008]

4.1.2 Need to enhance the walking environments

As may be understood, the city offers increased risks to the pedestrians, reasons being shared right-of-way, encroachment of footpaths, badly designed pedestrian paths and cycle tracks, lack of safe pedestrian crossing facilities at busy intersections, etc. Urban sprawl too has added to the woes of the non-motorized transport (NMT) modes. Pedestrian infrastructure is generally neglected and not given adequate focus in municipal planning and budgets. Many NMT commuters are forced to resort to motorized modes which are generally perceived safe. Still there are a huge number of commuters who because of their poor socio-economic status, walk for long distances and constantly struggle for space with the motorized traffic. This reduces the time and energy they can spend on productive activities. Further, in the context of the present socio-economic realities in most developing countries, pedestrians, cyclists and other slow-moving vehicles cannot be eliminated from the urban landscape (Tiwari, 2001). These facts indicate the need for creating better walking environment rather than shifting to other transport modes.

Above being a macro level study of the city that focused primarily upon the major road arteries, suitability of the walking environment needs to be assessed for the varied neighbourhoods as well. The benefits of walking especially for shorter distances are repeatedly being highlighted in various researches. Therefore it seems pertinent to analyse the neighbourhoods as regards the responsiveness of their built environments to the pedestrian context. The study is based on the premise that the physical attributes of neighbourhoods can influence walking behaviours.

4.2 Selecting Neighbourhoods of Amritsar City for Further Investigation

The historicity of Amritsar city that dates back to the 16th century has much influenced its physical growth and development. This has generated varied density patterns and neighbourhood typologies. Consequently, the city's gross population density of 71 persons per hectare (pph) does not find a uniform distribution. While the Walled City area is marked by very high population densities (> 300 pph) that may go as high as 740 pph, the area outside is mostly marked by medium (100–300 pph) to low (< 100 pph) densities (SAI, 2010). Accordingly, three broad density zones have been identified: high, medium and low.

- The Walled City, constituting 2.5 percent (350 hectares) of the area of the city (14,237 hectares) and housing almost 16 percent of the population, is clearly a high density zone. This area is marked by typical medieval character in terms of narrow streets, humane scale, traditional spaces like streets and squares, rich heritage of historic buildings, streetscape, etc. However, it is enormously marred by vehicle invasion, poor infrastructure and lack of open spaces. This area is fairly uniform in character.
- The area outside the Walled City witnesses growth and development in the post 19th century. This area may further be subdivided, because of distinct character, as that on the southern and northern sides of the railway track. The development on the south is absolutely haphazard, sub-standard and unplanned therefore rejected for the purpose of the study. The area north of the railway line till the bye-pass is characterized by both medium and low density zones, low-rise developments, planned interventions, quality socio-economic infrastructure, large open spaces and wide variety of neighbourhood typologies. Therefore, more case studies were picked up from here to represent this variation.

- The peri-urban area, that is the area beyond the northern bye pass and within the future urbanisable limits, is characterized by concentration of upcoming planned residential developments that offer low-densities, high quality infrastructure and promise of a quality life. The area has vast potential in the future and is the hotbed for private developers. Investigation of this zone from pedestrian perspective may signify the need for intervention into the existing system so that our new developments promote and revive the pedestrian spirits.

In the delineation of the study areas, there were two choices that emerged from past studies, namely, defined areas around a specific destination (e.g. school) or a group of destinations (e.g. commercial centre); or neighbourhoods defined by administrative or other boundaries. The latter was preferred because it was expected that the administratively defined neighbourhoods would offer some uniformity in built character and easy data availability.

The identified neighbourhoods were expected to represent the diversity in the city fully. The city has both the flatted and plotted type of housing developments; however, the latter dominate. Smaller sized neighbourhoods were generally avoided for selection. In addition to the above parameters, reconnaissance surveys and suggestions by the local associates implementing the survey also helped in identifying the neighbourhoods to be surveyed.

Case study areas hence shortlisted are briefed in Table 4.2. A total of 14 neighbourhoods were selected with boundaries demarcated based on Google maps. While twelve of these are fully developed, two (N-12 and N-14) are only partially developed. Two neighbourhoods, N-1 and N-2, represent the high densities of the walled city area. The area outside the walled city was too diversified in character making more number of case studies indispensable. Pedestrian-sensitive parameters need to be injected into the new developments. Therefore, the plan proposals of upcoming residential developments too need to be investigated to develop understanding of the latest trends. Holy city (N-14), an upcoming residential development that aggregates 11 licensed colonies, was considered for being the quintessence of many such developments, and was delineated based on the combined proposed layout plan. Spatial distribution of the neighbourhoods is depicted in Figure 4.3.

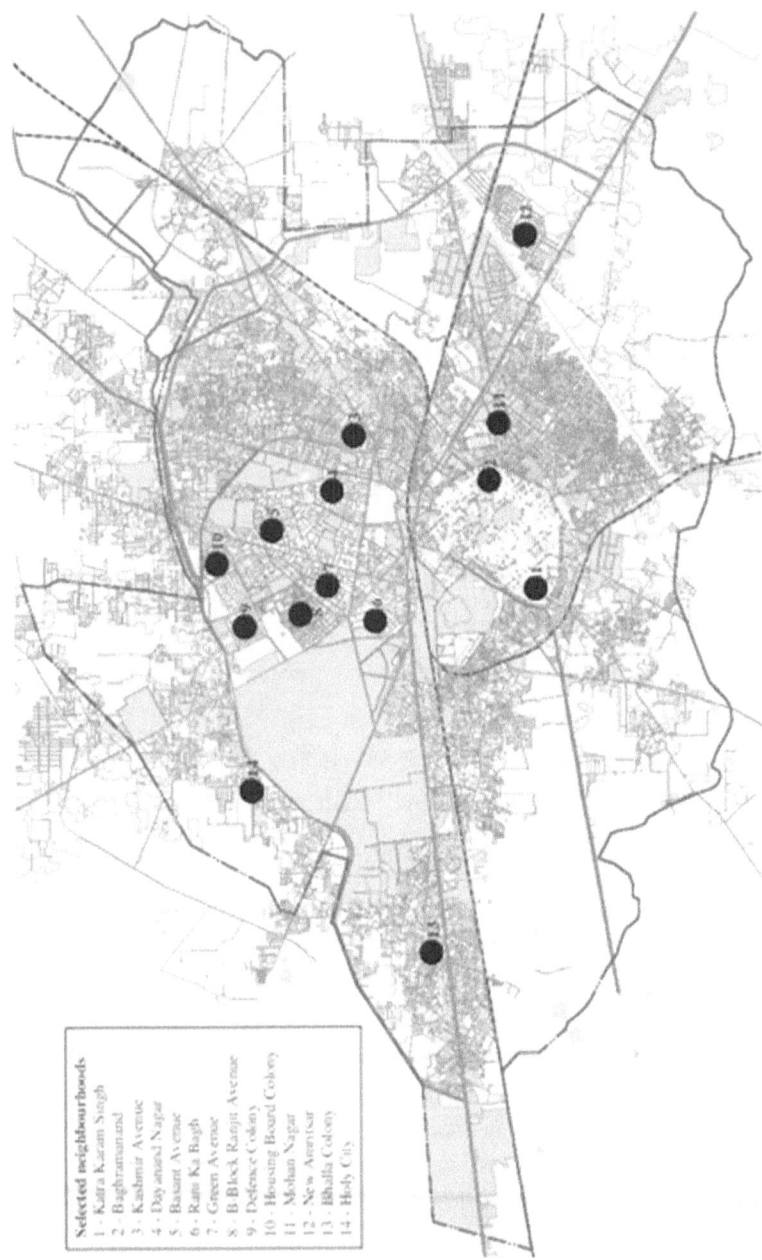

Figure 4.3 Spatial distribution of the selected neighbourhoods in Amritsar city [*Source*: Draft Master Plan of Amritsar (2010–31)]

Table 4.2 Neighbourhoods of Amritsar city selected for investigation

	Name of the neighbourhood	Density# as per Master Plan	Area (in acres)*	Neighbourhood Code
1	Katra Karam Singh	High	71.8	N-1
2	Bagh Ramanand	High	36.7	N-2
3	Kashmir Avenue	Medium	81.9	N-3
4	Dayanand Nagar	Low	67.0	N-4
5	Basant Avenue	Low	73.8	N-5
6	Rani Ka Bagh	Medium	112.2	N-6
7	Green Avenue	Low	144.4	N-7
8	B-block, Ranjit Avenue	Low	70.7	N-8
9	Defence Colony	Low	71.7	N-9
10	Housing Board Colony	Low	51.0	N-10
11	Mohan Nagar	High	52.1	N-11
12	New Amritsar	Low	264.3	N-12
13	Bhalla Colony	Low	47.7	N-13
14	Holy City	Low	94.0	N-14

*Values calculated based on Google Maps/ Proposed Layout Plan
#High (>300 pph); Medium (100–300 pph); Low (<100 pph)

4.3 Developing Framework for the Assessment of Neighbourhood Walkability

4.3.1 Previous and current trends of walkability assessment

Various researchers have attempted to study the influence of physical environment variables on walkability by considering the varied range of features – from a small subset to an entire comprehensive list. The variables, being large in number and too complicated and diverse in nature, do not offer themselves to a single method of query. While some aspects may be easily measured in objective terms, others are more subjective in their dispensation. Some features provide a macro-framework for analysis; the other features have to be investigated at a micro-level in the neighbourhood. It follows that two broad approaches, independently or in combination, have been adopted for measuring the pedestrian environment with each having its own set of benefits and limitations.

Objective assessment of neighbourhood environment: Large numbers of previous studies have sculpted the individual or group behaviours based on the selected few aspects of neighbourhood environment that could be measured objectively. The information for these aspects, namely, population or employment densities, land-use mix, street network connectivity and network densities, could be readily procured from secondary sources at a comprehensive spatial unit level (Clifton et al., 2007). Residential density is readily available from census data in many countries; land-use diversity becomes objectively implicit from field visits; and the characteristics such as street width, block size, presence of sidewalks and bike lanes, speed limits and public transit service may be observed and summarized for each neighbourhood (Sallis, 2009). Integration with GIS (geographic information system) technology has further widened the scope of objective assessment of the neighbourhood environment. The data can be collected automatically using GIS that may further be utilized in analyzing the street network characteristics such as measuring either block length or characterizing intersection type (Clifton, 2007). Thus the method saves time and resources, and may be applied to characterize large areas. The information generated may also assist the proposed designs (Parks and Schofer, 2006).

Clifton (2007) apprehended that the macro level features could not capture the multi-dimensional spirit of the physical environment that supported pedestrians, and therefore offered inconsistent and inappropriate environmental data. For reasons of the slow speed and nature of walking, a pedestrian is much more aware of and exposed to the physical environment than a driver, and observes its micro level details. Therefore, it is likely that the micro-features in the environment largely determine the pedestrian travel. Rundle et al. (2011) observes that such spatially referenced data is usually collected to meet local administrative priorities; is often inconsistently available or collected using different methodologies across jurisdictions; and often does not include many neighbourhood features of interest to researchers.

Subjective assessment of neighbourhood environment: At the micro level of walkability assessment, the information may be collected either by seeking residents' feedback or by members of a research team (Clifton et al, 2008). The feedback from the residents regarding perception of their neighbourhoods shall play a critical role in developing strategies for walkability enhancement. Residents may be expected to provide the most pertinent account of their needs and expectations from the built environment as also the neighbourhood walkability attributes. But since survey-based measures require field visits, therefore they are time-consuming and expensive to conduct largely due to the costs of travel. The huge amount of manpower and other resources that it entails makes it impracticable. It is not possible to use this method to characterize proposed designs (Parks and Schofer, 2006). Further, subjective responses of the residents are often inconsistent and prejudiced; and may misinform while conceptualizing any planning strategies. The limitation to some extent may be overcome by using multiple well-trained surveyors by the researchers. Rundle et al. (2011) inform that the current researches are increasingly based on neighbourhood audit tools that allow for a systematic observation of the area; define theoretically relevant measures; and attempt assessment of reliability and validity.

Audit tools for walkability assessment: Walking audit is "a tool used to inventory and assess physical environmental conditions associated with walking and bicycling" (Moudon and Lee, 2003). Walking audits often collect both quantitative and qualitative data about the physical and social environment that affect walking. Focused to consider and promote the needs of pedestrians as a form of transport, the walking audits may be undertaken by a range of different stakeholders including local community groups, transport planners or engineers, urban planners, urban designers and local politicians or councillors. For traffic engineers, planners and other decision makers, the simple but powerful tool would generate information that can help identify areas conducive to walking or needing changes; and create a platform for ushering in appropriate changes or improvements. These may also be used to analyze proposed development plans or other projects that intend to introduce changes into the physical environment. Pedestrian advocacy groups may use walk audits to generate understanding among community members for the pedestrian concerns.

There is a horde of walking audit tools, with most coming from United States or Australia. Determining which type of audit tool is most appropriate will depend on the audit participants, data needs and available resources. The different tools reflect a wide variation in the number of items being measured for the assessment of walkability (Su et al., 2014): The Irvine-Minnesota Inventory includes 162 items; Active Neighbourhood Checklist measures 89; Analytic Audit Tool measures 27 items; SPACES instrument 51; while Pedestrian Environment Data Scan (PEDS) tool measures only 36. Su et al. (2014) developed a 41-item urban built environment scan tool (CUBEST) for objective assessment of neighbourhood-built environment features related to physical activity in China. The number of items to be surveyed determines the time commitment expected out of the surveyors. As per an exhaustive analysis of audit instruments by Clifton et al. (2007), PEDS requires the least time of 3–5 minutes for auditing one segment or block compared to 10 minutes of Analytic Audit Tool and 20 minutes of Irvine-Minnesota Inventory.

An overview and comparison of three selected audit tools is provided in Table 4.3. It follows that while Pedestrian Environment Review System (PERS) is designed to be employed by Agencies and does not allow participation of end-users, it has the ability to be integrated with GIS; Neighbourhood Environment Walkability Scale (NEWS) seeks residents' feedback and is therefore absolutely subjective. PEDS combines subjective and objective assessment, and is comprehensive as regards the study aspects, but compact for ease of administering. This may easily be filled by a layman but with some training.

Table 4.3 Overview of selected pedestrian audit tools

	Pedestrian Environment Review System (PERS)	Neighbourhood Environment Walkability Scale (NEWS)	Pedestrian Environmental Data Scan (PEDS)
Relevant Organisations	• Transport Research Laboratory for Transport for London, England	• San Diego State University, USA	• University of Maryland & University of North Carolina, USA
Aim	• Systematic evaluation of the pedestrian environment • Holistic and objective tool for the local authorities to identify 'quality gaps' in the walking environment and prioritise funding	• Measure residents' perceptions about the neighbourhood environmental attributes • Develop the relation of perceived attributes to the frequency of walking trips for transport and recreation	• Capture street segments' built and natural environment features • Balance the need for detailed information about the environment with economy of administration

Cotd...

Cotd...

	Pedestrian Environment Review System (PERS)	**Neighbourhood Environment Walkability Scale (NEWS)**	**Pedestrian Environmental Data Scan (PEDS)**
Environmental Attributes	• Links (footways, subways and footbridges) • Crossings (formal and informal) • Routes (between key destinations) • Public transport waiting areas (bus stops, tram stops, taxi ranks) • Public spaces (squares and parks) • Interchange spaces (spaces between different modes)	• The 68 item instrument measures • Residential density • Proximity to non-residential land uses • Ease of access to non-residential uses • Street connectivity • Walking/cycling facilities • Aesthetics • Pedestrian traffic safety • Crime safety	• The single page audit instrument objectively assesses • Land use and street block environment, • Pedestrian facility • Road attributes • Walking/ cycling environment • Also includes 4 subjective evaluation items to rate the environment as a whole • In all, there are 40 questions, resulting in 83 measures
End User Involvement	• Transport agencies and local authorities involved with development and validation • Not end-user based	• Questionnaires seeking feedback of residents	• Designed to be administered by trained auditors in pairs • Free of planning jargon, the pencil-paper version may be filled by a layperson
Scoring System and Output Type	• Each facility rated on a seven point scale (–3 to +3) for different parameters • Ratings linked to red/ amber/ green or RAG (poor to good) colour-coding	• Items rated on a 4-point Likert Scale from 1 (strongly disagree) to 4 (strongly agree), except for aspects of residential density and land use mix diversity	• Provides a fine-grained inventory of the pedestrian environment, but does not feature any scoring system
Other Features	• PERS-3 software allows users to analyse and display walkability data using GIS maps, charts and quick win (low cost, easy to implement physical improvements) recommendation lists. • Ability to add photographs and geo-references of quick wins	• Provides multiple versions of the audit tool – one especially for parents, other for adolescents.	• Extensive and intensive training for the audit raters to ensure inter- and intra-rater reliability of the audit • A separate protocol providing detailed instructions for each audit item to ensure effective administration • Integration with handheld technology that ensures the ease of administration and improved quality of data

4.3.2 Identifying the parameters of study and survey process

Responsiveness of built environment to pedestrian concerns: Various pedestrian audits for investigating the built environments have been developed in the past. These are based on the ratings by trained raters, and provide fairly accurate assessment of the pedestrian environment at minimal time and cost. Initially inspired by the Pedestrian Environmental Data Scan (PEDS), the single page audit instrument developed by the University of Maryland and University of North Carolina, USA (Annexure-I), the survey format was modified to suit the Indian context. Reconnaissance surveys in the study area too were utilised to refine the Survey Performa. Consequently, the study of neighbourhood walkability was attempted both objectively and subjectively through seven broad parameters that comprised as many as 34 attributes (Table 4.4). Description of these is provided in Annexure II.

Table 4.4 Selected parameters and attributes of study

	Parameters of study	Attributes of study
I	General Street Environment	1. Street hierarchy 2. Types of buildings or land uses 3. Average building/ plot frontage 4. Connectivity
II	Pathway Availability and Quality	5. Type of pedestrian path 6. Path location 7. Path width 8. Kerb type 9. Path material 10. Path condition 11. Path continuity
III	Obstructions to Walking	12. Permanent obstructions 13. Temporary obstructions 14. On street parking scenario 15. Surface condition or maintenance
IV	Traffic Safety	16. Traffic volume 17. Posted speed limit 18. Number of traffic lanes 19. Crossing aids 20. Traffic calming devices
V	Disability Infrastructure	21. Any accessibility features

Contd...

	Parameters of study	Attributes of study
VI	Pedestrian Amenities	22. Availability of pedestrian amenities 23. Condition of pedestrian amenities 24. Location of pedestrian amenities 25. Signage and public art 26. Overall cleanliness/ maintenance 27. Street lighting 28. Availability of shade
VII	Spatial Quality	29. Building setbacks from sidewalk/ road edge 30. Building heights 31. Degree of enclosure 32. Articulation in building designs 33. Street orientation of buildings 34. Natural sights

Survey Performa was divided into a total of eight sections (Annexure-III). The first seven sections objectively assessed the walkability of a particular street segment through a total of 34 questions, before seeking subjective responses in the eighth section through 7 questions. The subjective responses were sought on a 5-point Likert Scale, and ranged from very bad to very good. As per McMilan et al. (2010), sampling 25% of the street or road segments may be enough to represent the walkability of a neighbourhood. Accordingly, 9–14 segments per neighbourhood were identified judiciously for the purpose of street-level walkability surveys, taking care that no street segment would go beyond the range of 50–400 meters.

The various parameters and attributes were analysed in terms of their prevalence at the overall city level. A total of 158 segments fairly distributed among 14 neighbourhoods (mean length 213.27 m; min. 52 m; max. 400 m; std. deviation 80.796) were considered for the purpose (Table 4.5).

Table 4.5 Number and length of segments surveyed in the selected neighbourhoods

	Name of the neighbourhood	Neighbourhood Code	No. of segments surveyed	Total length of segments surveyed (meters)
1	Katra Karam Singh	N-1	10	2011
2	Bagh Ramanand	N-2	12	2238
3	Kashmir Avenue	N-3	10	1938
4	Dayanand Nagar	N-4	11	2210

Contd...

Contd...

Name of the neighbourhood	Neighbourhood Code	No. of segments surveyed	Total length of segments surveyed (meters)
5 Basant Avenue	N-5	14	2957
6 Rani Ka Bagh	N-6	12	2336
7 Green Avenue	N-7	13	3808
8 B-block, Ranjit Avenue	N-8	14	3292
9 Defence Colony	N-9	12	2722
10 Housing Board Colony	N-10	10	2017
11 Mohan Nagar	N-11	10	1757
12 New Amritsar	N-12	10	1997
13 Bhalla Colony	N-13	11	1948
14 Holy City	N-14	9	2465
Grand total		**158**	**33696**

For the purpose of field survey, 10 undergraduate students of Architecture were selected who were passionate and could be keen observant by virtue of their profession. The survey team was subjected to rigorous pre-hand orientation to ensure objectivity and reliability of results. Various sessions in terms of discussions and presentations were conducted with the survey team. To overcome the limitation of subjectivity of seven questions, the Survey Performa was so prepared that the initial 34 objective questions subtly fine-tuned the surveyors' perception and understanding of the seven shortlisted aspects of pedestrian built environment. Further, surveying in pairs rather than singly was preferred for higher reliability.

Pedestrian perception and preference survey: Walkability is largely an outcome of individual preferences and socio-cultural perceptions. Most of the studies pertaining to walkability have thrived on residents' feedback. Though the residents' feedback may provide a very pertinent account of the situation, but these always had huge cost and time implications. Replication of such efforts would be too infuriating and cumbersome.

Pedestrian surveys were conducted in each of the selected neighbourhoods so as to capture the views and preferences of pedestrians. These were considered important since the proposed improvements must synchronize the expectations of the residents so as to ensure significant improvement in walkability trends in the future. Sample size was intentionally kept small as it was expected to provide reasonable accuracy within the constraints of time and cost. A short questionnaire on social characteristics and walkability preferences was designed based on previous studies (Annexure-IV).

(1) *Socio-economic profile*: This documented the social characteristics of the respondents in terms of gender, age, income and vehicle ownership. This was a prerequisite to understand their walkability preferences and the desired improvements.

(2) *Pedestrian preferences*: The respondents were explored for their perception of the walking environment, their latent desire to walk more as also their desired improvements in the neighbourhood built environment. For this, four questions were posed to them, with the former two on a 5-point Likert Scale. The respondents were first interrogated about their preference for walking over driving, with the options ranging from almost 'every time' to 'never'. The second question pertained to the rating of their neighbourhoods from pedestrian perspective, and sought their responses in terms of 'very good', 'good', 'average', 'bad' or 'very bad'. The pedestrians were further explored about their willingness to improve walk habits with the improved walkability conditions. The responses were sought on a four point Likert Scale in terms of 'certainly', 'may think', 'not at all' or 'don't know'. The fourth question specifically sought their desired improvements in the built environment for better walkability. A total of ten options were offered to them which they were required to rank as per their preference order.

The respondents were offered the choice of questionnaire in English or Punjabi to overcome any language handicap. As many as 218 pedestrians were interviewed in the various selected neighbourhoods with a sample size of 13–20 respondents per neighbourhood. This ensured feedback from diverse set of people. The data procured was then aggregated for the whole city.

Audit protocol: The surveyors were equipped with the following as they set out for the audit:
- City map identifying the location and boundaries of the neighbourhood

- Neighbourhood map denoted with the street segment numbers
- Copies of the Performa for field survey of segment level parameters
- Copies of the questionnaire for pedestrian perception and preference survey
- Measuring tape or a distance measuring device
- Cellular phone/ digital camera

Upon entering a street segment, the surveyor first noted on the Performa, the segment number as it corresponded to the neighbourhood segment map as also the date and time. The protocol expected that the surveyor would walk the segment once to get a feel of the surroundings, and then would walk again while filling out the Survey Performa. However, after surveying a few segments, the surveyors found it more efficient to fill out the Survey Performa simultaneous to their first walk. It took approximately five minutes to ten minutes to administer the audit for each segment. Due to the large number of attributes, one could inadvertently skip over some questions. So the Performa was verified for completeness before moving on to the next segment. Surveyors ensured that the Performa for pedestrian perception and preference survey also got filled as and when they encountered any neighbourhood resident. This ensured residents' feedbacks from diverse settings.

Both the field walkability survey and the pedestrian interview survey were undertaken simultaneously and mostly conducted from 2:00 p.m. to 5:00 p.m. during the months of October to February for reasons of weather comfort.

Data compilation and analysis: The data were coded, entered and checked utilizing MS Excel and IBM SPSS Statistics 21. Each of the parameters and attributes of study was subjected to rigorous analysis for each neighbourhood as also cumulatively for the whole city. The desired end product of the study is walkability score for each neighbourhood that need to be compared and interpreted in respect of the various aspects. Therefore, maximum scores were fixed for the various walkability parameters and attributes (Annexure V).

The score attained for a parameter is the summation of weighted average scores of the various attributes categorized under that. The walkability score of a particular neighbourhood is the summation of respective scores for all its parameters. Weights were assigned to the probable responses based on their impact on walkability derived from past studies (Annexure-V). Based on the assigned weights, weighted average scores for each of the attributes at cumulative level were calculated as under:

$$(WA_i) = \frac{(\Sigma R_i \times N_i)}{\Sigma N_i}$$

where WA represents the weighted average score for an attribute, R represents the weights assigned to the various probable responses to a particular attribute and N represents the frequency of occurrence of such responses.

These scores were then subjected to Analysis of Variance (ANOVA) to understand and interpret their variability based on broad population density categories. The post-hoc tests were undertaken to determine the direction of variability of the mean scores.

The data collected from residents of various neighbourhoods ensured feedback from diverse set of residents that was subsequently utilized to generate information at cumulative city level as regards the residents' perceptions and preferences for improvements. This was important for determining their acceptability for any improvement initiatives.

The data were coded, entered and checked utilizing MS Excel and IBM SPSS Statistics 21. Chi-square tests were performed to measure association of the pedestrian preferences with socio-economic characteristics of the respondents, and further crosstab test measured the degree of association of the shortlisted characteristics.

The rankings provided by the 218 resident respondents to the desired improvements are compiled in Table 4.7, and the weighted averages for each of the desired improvements were calculated as under:

$$(WA_i) = \frac{(\Sigma R_i \times N_i)}{\Sigma N_i}$$

where WA represents the weighted average for the desired improvement, R represents the allocated score for a particular rank and N represents the number of respondents. The score allocated for 1st rank is 10, 2nd rank is 9 and so on up to 10th rank with score of 1.

Walk Scenario in the Neighbourhoods of Amritsar City: A Case Study

Figure 4.4 Glimpses of 'general street environment' in the neighbourhoods of Amritsar city

Figure 4.5 Glimpses of 'pathway availability and quality' in the neighbourhoods of Amritsar city

Walk Scenario in the Neighbourhoods of Amritsar City: A Case Study 85

Figure 4.6 Glimpses of 'obstructions to walking' in the neighbourhoods of Amritsar city

86   Towards Pedestrian-Friendly Neighbourhoods

Figure 4.7 Glimpses of 'traffic safety' in the neighbourhoods of Amritsar city

Figure 4.8 Glimpses of 'pedestrian amenities' in the neighbourhoods of Amritsar city

Figure 4.9 Glimpses of 'spatial quality' in the neighbourhoods of Amritsar city

4.4 Observations Regarding Responsiveness of Neighbourhood Built Environment to the Pedestrian Concerns

4.4.1 Prevalence of various attributes in the neighbourhoods

The prevalence of various attributes of the seven parameters is provided in Table 4.4. Figures 4.4 to 4.9 capture the glimpses, from the perspective of these parameters, of the neighbourhood streets of Amritsar city.

General street environment: It is observed that of the total 158 segments, most (79.1 percent) belong to access street category, followed by the collector streets (14.6 percent). As regards the types of buildings or land uses, most of the streets have residential plotted developments (83.5 percent), while only 14.6 percent have residential flatted developments. The mixed use plots could be found in 22.8 percent of the street segments. Of the land uses that are conducive to walking, recreational is the most prevalent (17.7 percent). Of the deterrents, vacant/undeveloped lots take the larger toll (15.8 percent; Figure 4.10). As regards the plot frontages, most streets have plots with moderate frontages (47.5 percent) with almost equal percentage of plots with narrow frontages (46.2 percent). Segment connectivity is most prevalent in the category of 4–6 (49.4 percent), but since the segments vary widely in their lengths, so this attribute cannot be conclusive.

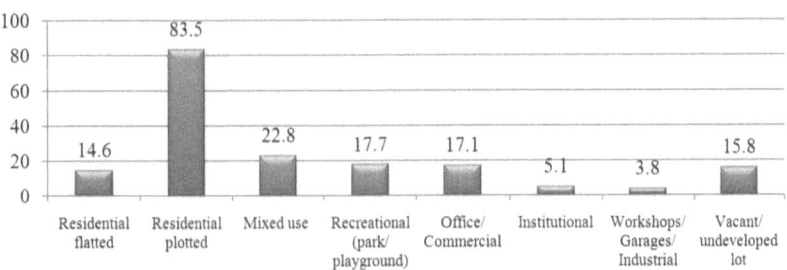

Figure 4.10 Prevalence (percent) of various types of buildings/ land uses

Pathway availability and quality: It is observed that of the total 158 segments, 49.4 percent segments lack any clearly defined space for the pedestrians, 15.8 percent segments comprise of worn dirt paths leaving only 22.2 percent segments provided with sidewalks (Figure 4.11).

Of the total 60 segments having sidewalks or worn dirt footpaths, 90 percent segments have pedestrian paths just next to the road kerb. Of the 80 various pedestrian path categories, width from 1.2 m to 1.8 m is the most prevalent (47.5 percent). Most of these paths (72.5 percent) have no kerbs (Figure 4.12); however, precast pavers or stone paving form the most prevalent (61.3 percent) path material. The paths are mostly intermittent (62.5 percent) to the discomfort of most users.

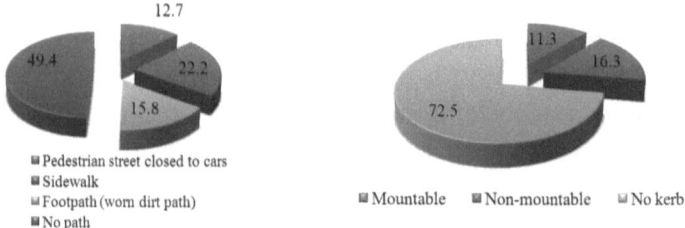

Figure 4.11 Prevalence (percent) of various types of pedestrian paths

Figure 4.12 Prevalence (percent) of various kerb types

Obstructions to walking: The most prominent of the walking obstructions observed in various neighbourhood streets of Amritsar are the parked vehicles that prevail on 73.4 percent of the streets, followed by poles, mesh of wires, etc. (60.1 percent; Figure 4.13). However, the parked vehicles remain in moderate numbers covering not more than 1/3rd of the street facade on 73.4 percent of the streets where they exist. Parked vehicles dominate on 19.6 percent of the streets. Trees, shrubs, bushes, etc., create obstructions on 51.9 percent of the streets. The surface conditions have been found moderate on 58.9 percent of the streets while 29.1 percent streets seem to be in poor condition or undergoing repair works.

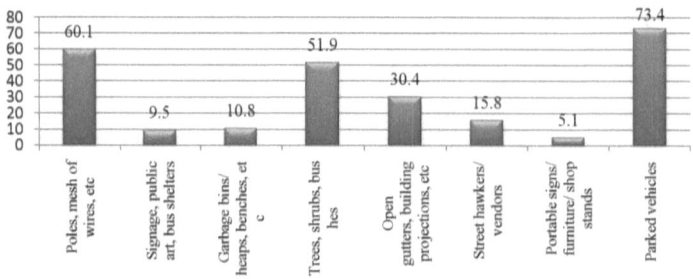

Figure 4.13 Prevalence (percent) of various permanent and temporary obstructions

Traffic safety: It is observed that 48.7 percent of the neighbourhood streets in Amritsar have medium traffic followed by 38.6 percent streets that evidenced low to very low traffic volume. However, the traffic volume would show lots of variations based on the time of the day and weather conditions. The speed limit however has not been posted anywhere on the access streets, collectors or sub-arterials. In most cases (86.7 percent), the traffic lanes are not many. Of the various crossing aids and traffic calming devices, speed bumps seem to be the only devices utilised but only on 36.1 percent of the neighbourhood streets. Zebra crossings are found on a mere 3.8 percent of the streets. Median refuge or traffic island and the pedestrian signals are conspicuous by their complete absence in the city (Figure 4.14). While these may be considered as the elements of Western culture, these provide direction and offer some potential for improvement of neighbourhood streets of Amritsar city.

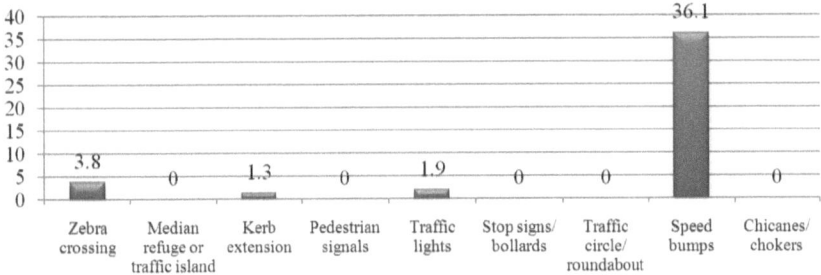

Figure 4.14 Prevalence (percent) of various crossing aids and traffic-calming devices

Disability infrastructure: There is absolutely no consideration for the disabled as evident from the absence of any such features. The Disability (Equal Opportunities, Protection of Rights and Full Participation) Act of 1995 of the Public Works Department provides for non-discrimination in the access to the built environment. The Section 45 of the Act makes certain elements and features of universal design mandatory like installation of auditory signals at red lights on public roads for the benefit of persons with visual handicap, curb cuts and slopes for easy access of wheel chair users, engraving on the surface of the zebra crossing for the blind or the persons with lower vision (CSE, 2009). But this has not been implemented and walking in the Amritsar neighbourhoods remains absolutely inaccessible and unsafe.

Pedestrian amenities: Of the various possible pedestrian amenities, it is observed that the garbage bins appear along 12.7 percent streets followed by street vendors along 10.1 percent streets (Figure 4.15). Only 35 of the 158 street segments (22.15 percent) had any pedestrian amenity available. Of these 35 segments, 48.6 percent segments have non-functional or poorly functional pedestrian amenities, while 60 percent segments find them obstructing the pedestrian movement. Signage and public art is negligible. The streets have been found to be performing fairly (70.3 percent) as regards overall cleanliness/ maintenance (litter, rubbish, graffiti, etc.). Street lighting is found mainly for the benefit of the motorists and is road oriented in 63.9 percent of the streets. The pedestrian realm seems to get the benefit of street lights only in 17.7 percent cases. Further, the shade whether from buildings or trees too is mostly intermittent (54.4 percent). It is observed that there is almost complete disregard for the *pedestrian amenities* in the neighbourhood streets of Amritsar city.

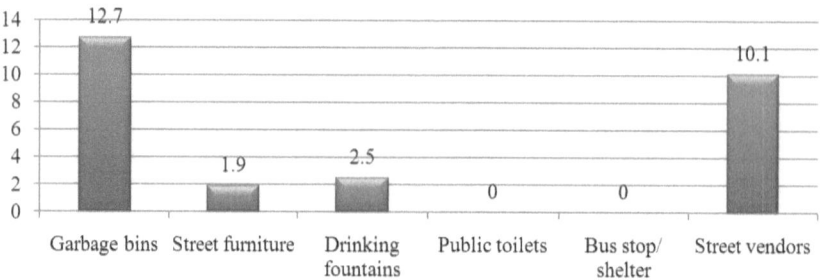

Figure 4.15 Prevalence (percent) of various pedestrian amenities

Spatial quality: It is observed that buildings stand within a distance of 6 m from sidewalk or road edge in as many as 52.5 percent of the neighbourhood streets of Amritsar city, while they stand at the road edge in 44.3 percent cases. Buildings are mostly 1–2 storeyed along as many as 67.7 percent streets and 3–4 storeyed along 31.6 percent streets. This depicts a general trend of medium- to low-rise developments in Amritsar city. Most streets (54.4 percent) offer some sense of enclosure due to buildings or trees to the pedestrians. 23.4 percent streets offer little or no enclosure while 22.2 percent streets provide high sense of enclosure. Some articulation in building facades is evidenced in 58.2

percent of the streets followed by 22.8 percent of the streets with high articulation of building designs. Moderate level of openings is found in 51.9 percent of the streets followed by 34.8 percent streets offering lot many windows or porches or entrances (Figure 4.16). This signifies the visual penetrability of the neighbourhood streets for the benefit of the pedestrian. 51.3 percent of the streets offer moderate level of greenery intermittently placed, while 34.2 percent streets offer absolutely no natural attractions to the pedestrians (Figure 4.17).

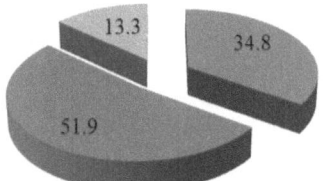

■ Lot many windows/ porches/ entrances
■ Moderate level of openings
■ Long dead facades/ boundary walls

Figure 4.16 Prevalence (percent) of street orientation of buildings

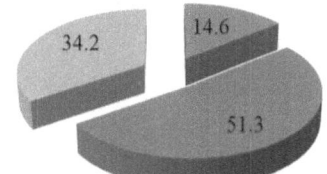

■ Lot of greenery offering visual continuity
■ Moderate level of greenery, intermittent placement
■ Absolutely no natural attractions

Figure 4.17 Prevalence (percent) of natural sights

4.4.2 Subjective assessment on a 5-point Likert Scale

The various parameters at segment level were observed from subjective point of view as well. The importance of visual perception of the environment cannot be denied in spite of having observed these objectively. On a five-point Likert Scale, the trained raters were asked to rate the pedestrian responsiveness of the 158 street segments through seven parameters. The results are provided in Table 4.6 and Figure 4.18.

Table 4.6 Subjective assessment of street segments in selected neighbourhoods

	Parameters		Very Bad	Bad	Average	Good	Very Good	Total
A	General street environment	Count	10	33	75	36	4	158
		Percent	6.3	20.9	47.5	22.8	2.5	100
B	Pathway availability and quality	Count	62	49	37	10	0	158
		Percent	39.2	31.0	23.4	6.3	0.0	100
C	Obstructions to walking	Count	44	69	40	5	0	158
		Percent	27.8	43.7	25.3	3.2	0.0	100

Contd...

Contd...

	Parameters		Very Bad	Bad	Average	Good	Very Good	Total
D	Traffic safety	Count	44	63	45	6	0	158
		Percent	27.8	39.9	28.5	3.8	0.0	100
E	Disability infrastructure	Count	147	11	0	0	0	158
		Percent	93.0	7.0	0.0	0.0	0.0	100
F	Pedestrian amenities	Count	99	46	10	3	0	158
		Percent	62.7	29.1	6.3	1.9	0.0	100
G	Spatial quality	Count	18	50	75	15	0	158
		Percent	11.4	31.6	47.5	9.5	0.0	100

[*Source*: Author's calculations]

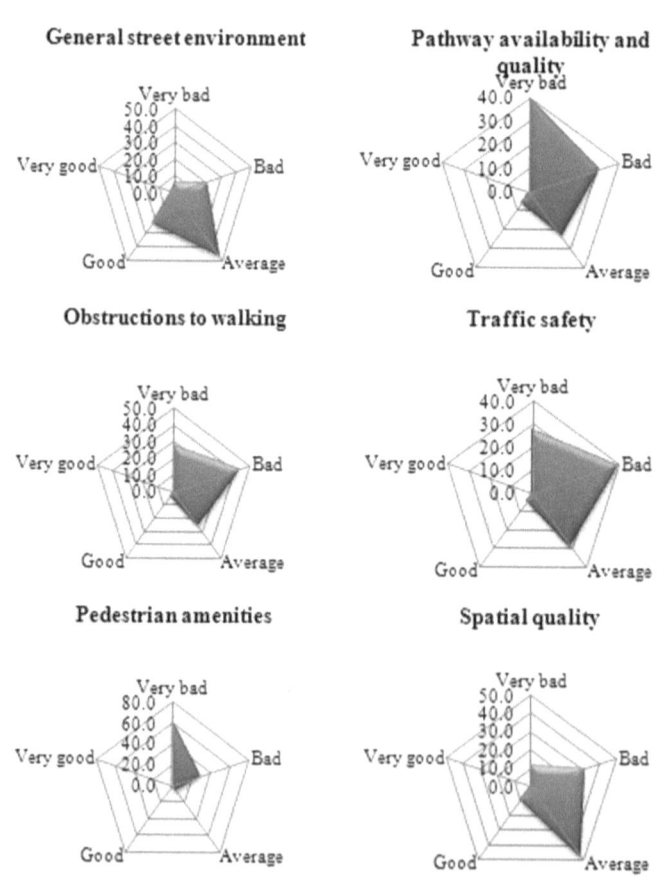

Figure 4.18 Subjective assessment (percent) of street segments in the selected neighbourhoods

It is observed that the parameter of *general street environment* has been rated as average in as many as 47.5 percent street segments, good in 22.8 percent segments and bad in 20.9 percent street segments. The parameter of *pathway availability and quality* is very bad in 39.2 percent cases, followed by bad in 31.0 percent cases. As many as 43.7 percent streets are bad in terms of *obstructions to walking*. *Traffic safety* has been found to be bad along 39.9 percent streets, average along 28.5 percent streets and very bad along 27.8 percent streets. *Disability infrastructure* is very bad along almost 93.0 percent neighbourhood streets. *Pedestrian amenities* have been rated very bad along as many as 62.7 percent street segments. *Spatial quality* is found average in 47.5 percent cases. On the whole, the general impression of neighbourhood streets of Amritsar city is found to fall between average and very bad, with good and very good categories showing negligible responses.

4.4.3 Developing walkability scores for neighbourhoods

Walkability scores for the various neighbourhoods were developed by way of aggregating the weighted average scores of all the parameters; while the walkability score for each of the parameters is the summation of weighted average scores of all its attributes.

General street environment: It is observed that the scores for *general street environment* of neighbourhoods fall within a narrow range from 8.09 to 10.30 reflecting a fairly uniform character as related to this parameter. *Segment type (A1)* attains a score of 3.0 in N-12 (New Amritsar) reflecting all segments falling in access street category. The attribute of *types of buildings/ land uses (A2)* finds the highest score of 2.20 for N-1 (Katra Karam Singh) reflecting a fair mix of compatible land uses in this neighbourhood. On the other extreme, N-14 (Holy City) attains the minimum score of 0.11 reflecting the prevalence of vacant/undeveloped plots. This is obviously because of partially developed status of this neighbourhood. The attribute of *average building/ plot frontage (A3)* gets full score for N-2 (Bagh Ramanand) and N-10 (Housing Board Colony) showing that these neighbourhoods are dominated by plots with narrow frontages. N-14 (Holy City) gets the lowest score of 1.89 followed by N-9 (Defence Colony) that gets 1.92. This shows the prevalence of large-sized plots in these neighbourhoods. The attribute of *segment connectivity (A4)* cannot be consequential because of the large range in segment lengths, hence ignored (Figure 4.19).

Pathway availability and quality: It is observed that the scores for neighbourhoods vary from absolute zero to 12.64 representing very poor to average condition of *pathway availability and quality*. While the zero score of N-2 (Bagh Ramanand) and N-13 (Bhalla Colony) represent an absolute negation of this walkability parameter, the highest value of 12.64 for N-5 (Basant Avenue) followed by 10.90 for N-12 (New Amritsar) highlights the apathy at the overall city level itself. Both N-5 (Basant Avenue) and N-12 (New Amritsar) score high under the attribute of *path material (B9)* which signifies the use of precast pavers/ stone paving as the path material (Figure 4.20).

Obstructions to walking: It is observed that the scores for neighbourhoods as regards *obstructions to walking* vary from 0.33 to 2.40 representing not much of the diversity. While N-10 (Housing Board Colony) has the best score of 2.40 followed by a substantial gap from the rest, N-2 (Bagh Ramanand) gets the worst score of 0.33. *Permanent obstructions (C12)* with scores of −2.60 and −2.30 dominate in N-12 (New Amritsar) and N-3 (Kashmir Avenue), respectively. *Temporary obstructions (C13)* with score of −2.00 dominate in N-1 (Katra Karam Singh). *On street parking (C14)* presents the worst scenario in N-4 (Dayanand Nagar) with value of 1.27, and is the best in N-9 (Defence Colony) with value 2.20 followed by N-12 (New Amritsar) with value 2.25. Maximum score for *surface conditions or the maintenance (C15)* is attained by N-11 (Mohan Nagar) and N-12 (New Amritsar) with value being 2.10 (Figure 4.21).

Traffic safety: It is observed that the scores for neighbourhoods fall within a very narrow range of 5.75–7.10 representing negligible diversity as regards this parameter. *Traffic volume (D16)* presents a pleasant picture for N-13 (Bhalla Colony) and N-14 (Holy City) with values of 2.73 and 2.67, respectively. However, the traffic volume presents variations based on the hour of the day, day of the week as also seasons. The *speed limit (D17)* is not posted on any of the neighbourhood streets. *Number of traffic lanes to be crossed (D18)* depicts the hierarchical status of streets at the city level. All neighbourhoods score badly for *crossing aids (D19)* as also for *traffic calming devices (D20)* (Figure 4.22).

Disability infrastructure: *Disability infrastructure* is extremely bad in the neighbourhoods of Amritsar city and calls for attention.

Pedestrian amenities: It is observed that the scores for neighbourhoods fall within a narrow range of 4.44–8.42 representing very little diversity as regards this parameter. While N-9 (Defence Colony) gets the highest score of 8.42 followed by N-1 (Katra Karam Singh) with 8.30 score, the lowest score of 4.70 goes for N-11 (Mohan Nagar). On closer scrutiny, it is found that N-4 (Dayanand Nagar), N-11 (Mohan Nagar), N-13 (Bhalla Colony) and N-14 (Holy City) are absolutely devoid of any pedestrian amenities. *Signage and public art (F25)* is also missing in most of the neighbourhoods. *Overall cleanliness in terms of litter, rubbish, graffiti, etc. (F26)* is the best in N-12 (New Amritsar) and N-4 (Dayanand Nagar) with scores as 2.10 and 2.09, respectively. *Street lighting (F27)* is mostly road oriented with highest score of 1.73 for N-4 (Dayanand Nagar). As regards *availability of shade whether from trees or buildings (F28)*, N-2 (Bagh Ramanand) scores the highest followed by N-1 (Katra Karam Singh) and N-10 (Housing Board Colony) with scores as 2.92 for the former and 2.80 for the latter two (Figure 4.23).

Spatial quality: It is observed that the scores for neighbourhoods fall within a narrow range of 10.55–13.58 representing very little diversity as regards this parameter. The highest score of 13.58 is attained by N-2 (Bagh Ramanand) followed by score of 13.30 by N-1 (Katra Karam Singh). The lowest score of 10.55 goes for N-13 (Bhalla Colony). Further, it is observed that as regards *building setbacks (G29)*, N-2 (Bagh Ramanand) and N-13 (Bhalla Colony) share the perfect score of 3.00, while lowest score of 1.89 is attained by N-14 (Holy City). *Building heights (G30)* has the highest scores in N-1 (Katra Karam Singh) and N-2 (Bagh Ramanand) with values of 1.93 and 1.83 respectively, and lowest score of value 1.00 in N-11 (Mohan Nagar), N-12 (New Amritsar) and N-13 (Bhalla Colony). *Degree of enclosure due to buildings or trees (G31)* again scores the highest in N-1 (Katra Karam Singh) and N-2 (Bagh Ramanand) with values 3.00 and 2.67, respectively. It is strange to find that *articulation in building designs (G32)* gets the highest scores in N-2 (Bagh Ramanand) and N-3 (Kashmir Avenue). Street orientation of buildings (G33) is found to be the best in N-12 (New Amritsar) followed by N-4 (Dayanand Nagar) with scores as 2.70 and 2.64, respectively. *Natural sights (G34)* have received highest scores in N-8 (B-block, Ranjit Avenue) and N-12 (New Amritsar), and the lowest in N-1 (Katra Karam Singh) and N-2 (Bagh Ramanand) (Figure 4.24).

Subjective assessment: The *subjective assessment* shows highest scores of 5.14 and 5.00 for N-14 (Holy City) and N-9 (Defence Colony) respectively, and the lowest score of 2.84 for N-2 (Bagh Ramanand). Of the various parameters, *general street environment (A)* gets the best city average score of 2.94 followed by *spatial quality (G)* that gets a city average of 2.55. *Disability infrastructure (E)* being conspicuous by its complete absence gets the least score. *Pedestrian amenities (F)* too are poor. However, the deficiencies highlight the potential aspects the betterment of which may significantly enhance the walkability of the neighbourhoods of Amritsar city (Figure 4.25).

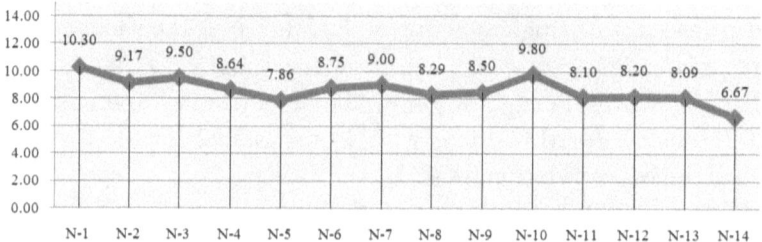

Figure 4.19 Objectively assessed walkability scores for general street environment

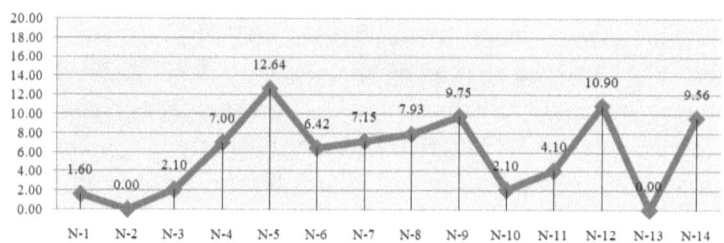

Figure 4.20 Objectively assessed walkability scores for pathway availability and quality

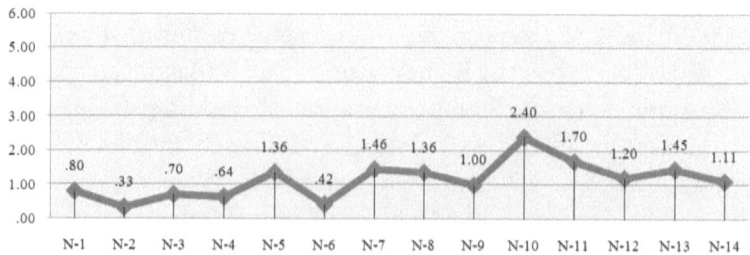

Figure 4.21 Objectively assessed walkability scores for obstructions to walking

Walk Scenario in the Neighbourhoods of Amritsar City: A Case Study

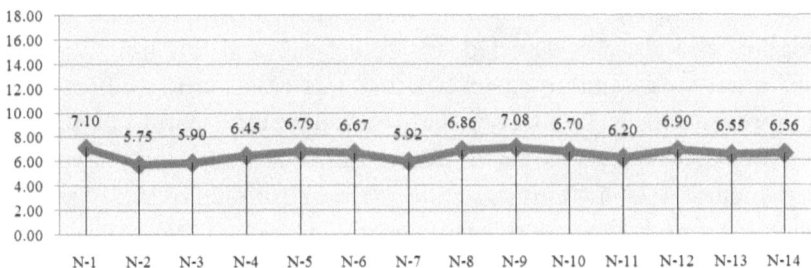

Figure 4.22 Objectively assessed walkability scores for traffic safety

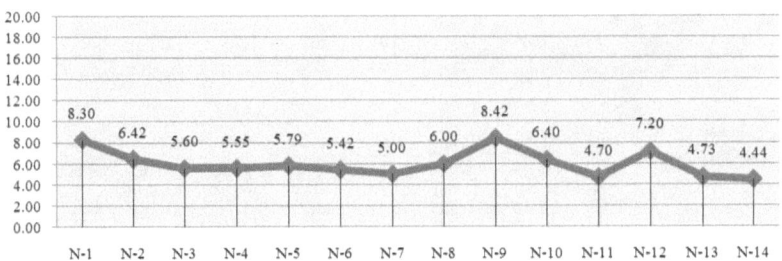

Figure 4.23 Objectively assessed walkability scores for pedestrian amenities

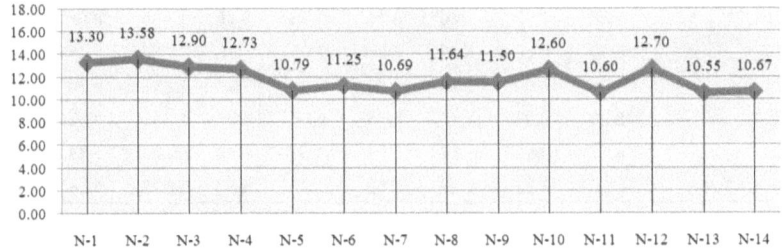

Figure 4.24 Objectively assessed walkability scores for spatial quality

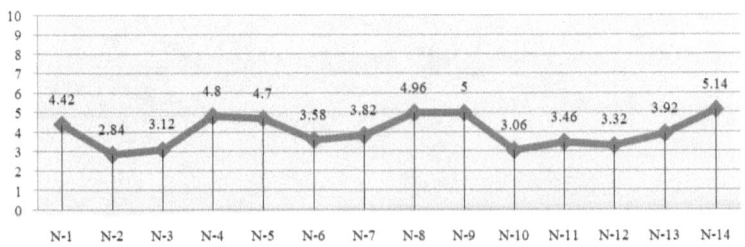

Figure 4.25 Walkability scores based on subjective assessment

Overall walkability scores: Overall walkability scores for the various neighbourhoods are depicted in Table 4.7 and Figure 4.26. The maximum value amounted to 110 that was adjusted to 100 for easier comprehension. It is observed that the walkability scores fall within a narrow range of 32.08–46.59 for the various neighbourhoods in Amritsar city. Figures 4.27–4.40 illustrate the attributes of each of the 14 selected neighbourhoods through relevant street sections and photographs.

Table 4.7 Overall walkability scores based on segment-level parameters

Attribute/ Neighbourhood Code	Walkability scores for various parameters								Overall score (100)
	A (15)	B (20)	C (6)	D (18)	E (3)	F (20)	G (18)	H (10)	
N-1	10.30	1.60	0.80	7.10	0.00	8.30	13.30	4.42	41.65
N-2	9.17	0.00	0.33	5.75	0.00	6.42	13.58	2.84	34.63
N-3	9.50	2.10	0.70	5.90	0.00	5.60	12.90	3.12	36.20
N-4	8.64	7.00	0.64	6.45	0.00	5.55	12.73	4.80	41.65
N-5	7.86	12.64	1.36	6.79	0.00	5.79	10.79	4.70	45.39
N-6	8.75	6.42	0.42	6.67	0.00	5.42	11.25	3.58	38.65
N-7	9.00	7.15	1.46	5.92	0.00	5.00	10.69	3.82	39.13
N-8	8.29	7.93	1.36	6.86	0.00	6.00	11.64	4.96	42.76
N-9	8.50	9.75	1.00	7.08	0.00	8.42	11.50	5.00	46.59
N-10	9.80	2.10	2.40	6.70	0.00	6.40	12.60	3.06	39.15
N-11	8.10	4.10	1.70	6.20	0.00	4.70	10.60	3.46	35.33
N-12	8.20	10.90	1.20	6.90	0.00	7.20	12.70	3.32	45.84
N-13	8.09	0.00	1.45	6.55	0.00	4.73	10.55	3.92	32.08
N-14	6.67	9.56	1.11	6.56	0.00	4.44	10.67	5.14	40.14
City average	8.63	5.99	1.13	6.53	0.00	6.00	11.78	4.04	40.09

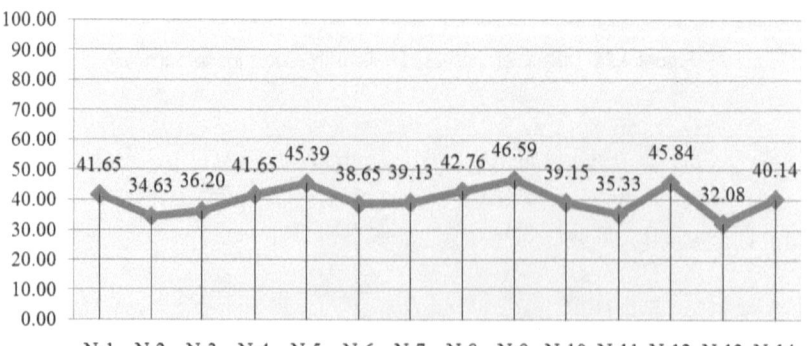

Figure 4.26 Overall walkability scores based on segment level parameters

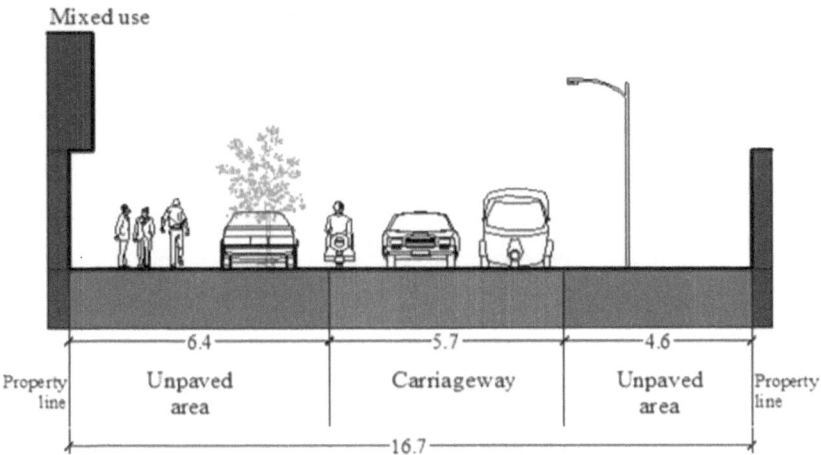

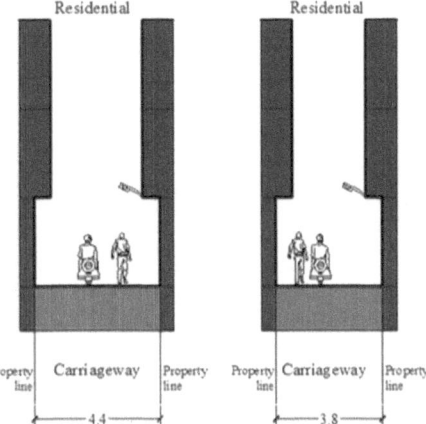

- Mixed traffic conditions
- Moderate to narrow building frontages
- High sense of enclosure along narrow streets
- No setbacks with buildings abutting the carriageway
- Continuous shade of buildings for pedestrian comfort along narrow streets
- Absolutely no natural sights of greenery
- Electricity poles, short ramps and other building projections create obstructions
- Hawkers, portable signs, parked vehicles, etc., as temporary obstructions
- Surface conditions optimum to poor

Figure 4.27 Street sections and pedestrian scenario in Katra Karam Singh (N-1)

102 Towards Pedestrian-Friendly Neighbourhoods

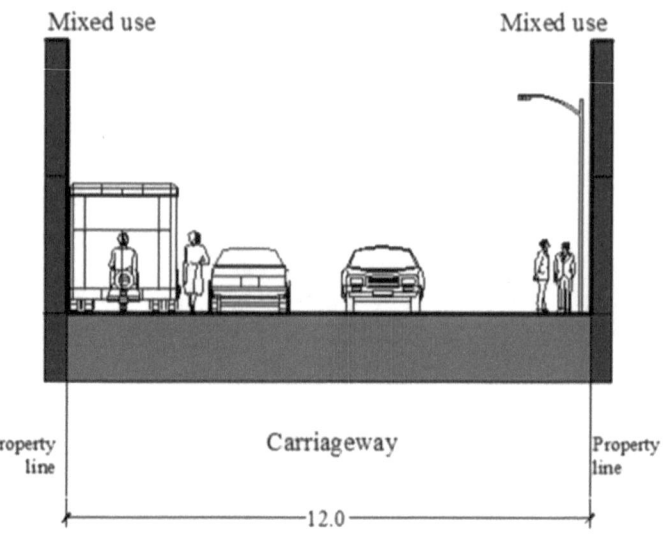

- Mixed traffic conditions
- Moderately to poorly articulated building facades
- High sense of enclosure along narrow streets
- No setbacks with buildings abutting the carriageway
- Continuous shade of buildings along narrow streets
- Sights of greenery grossly lacking
- Ramps and otherbuilding projections create obstructions
- Hawkers, parked vehicles, etc.,as temporary obstructions
- Surface conditions optimum with some streets provided with concrete pavers

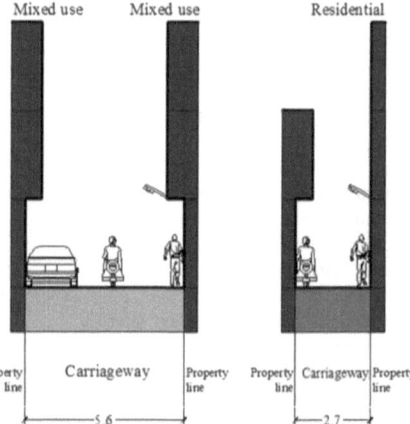

Figure 4.28 Street sections and pedestrian scenario in Bagh Ramanand (N-2)

Walk Scenario in the Neighbourhoods of Amritsar City: A Case Study 103

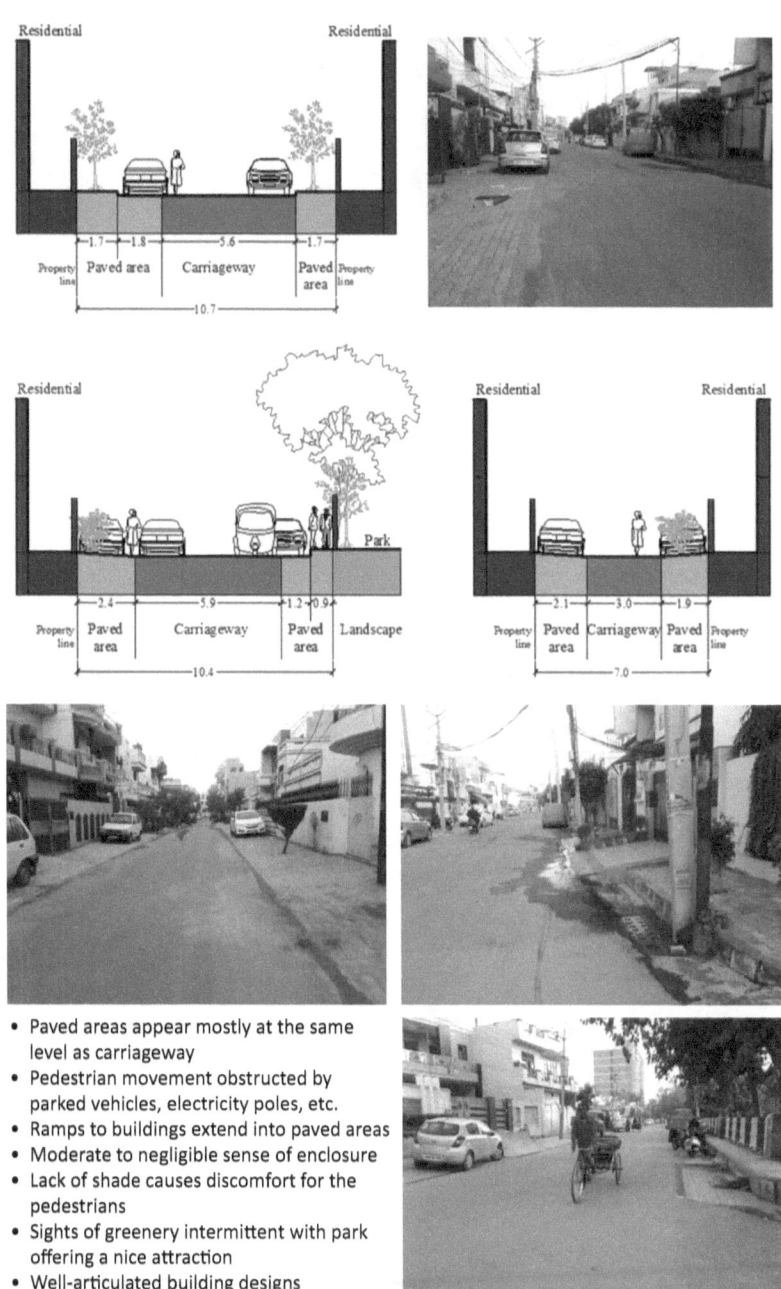

- Paved areas appear mostly at the same level as carriageway
- Pedestrian movement obstructed by parked vehicles, electricity poles, etc.
- Ramps to buildings extend into paved areas
- Moderate to negligible sense of enclosure
- Lack of shade causes discomfort for the pedestrians
- Sights of greenery intermittent with park offering a nice attraction
- Well-articulated building designs
- Good surface conditions

Figure 4.29 Street sections and pedestrian scenario in Kashmir Avenue (N-3)

104   Towards Pedestrian-Friendly Neighbourhoods

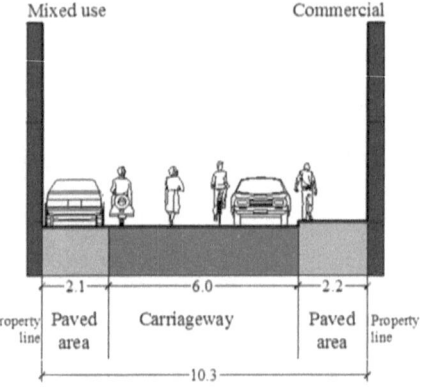

- Raised paved areas for pedestrian movement along certain streets
- Fully paved streets slows down the speeding vehicles
- Mixed use add vibrancy to the streets
- Moderate sense of enclosure
- Limited sights of greenery
- Entry ramps often extend into the street
- Moderately articulated building designs
- Piled up construction material, parked vehicles, etc., as pedestrian obstructions

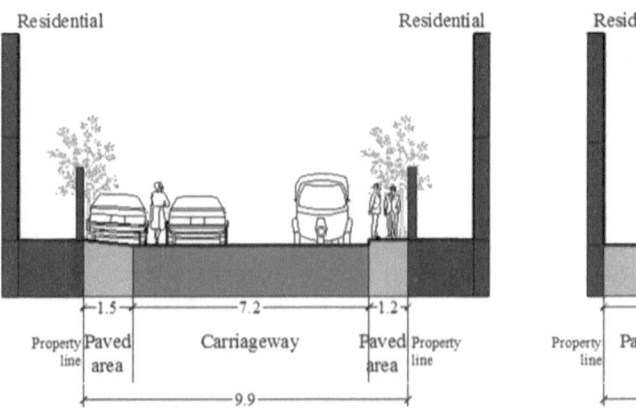
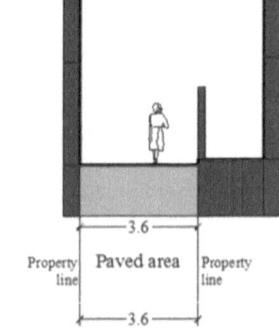

Figure 4.30 Street sections and pedestrian scenario in Dayanand Nagar (N-4)

Walk Scenario in the Neighbourhoods of Amritsar City: A Case Study 105

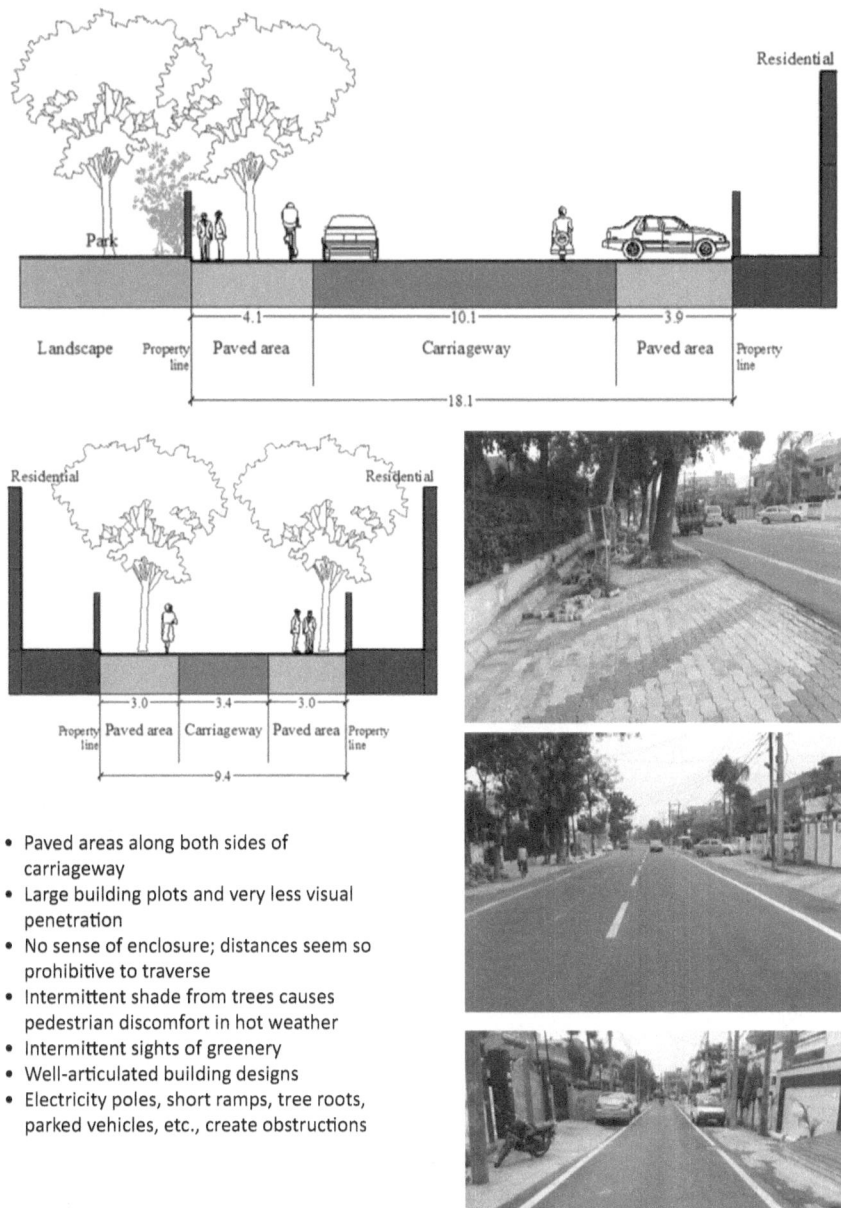

- Paved areas along both sides of carriageway
- Large building plots and very less visual penetration
- No sense of enclosure; distances seem so prohibitive to traverse
- Intermittent shade from trees causes pedestrian discomfort in hot weather
- Intermittent sights of greenery
- Well-articulated building designs
- Electricity poles, short ramps, tree roots, parked vehicles, etc., create obstructions

Figure 4.31 Street sections and pedestrian scenario in Basant Avenue (N-5)

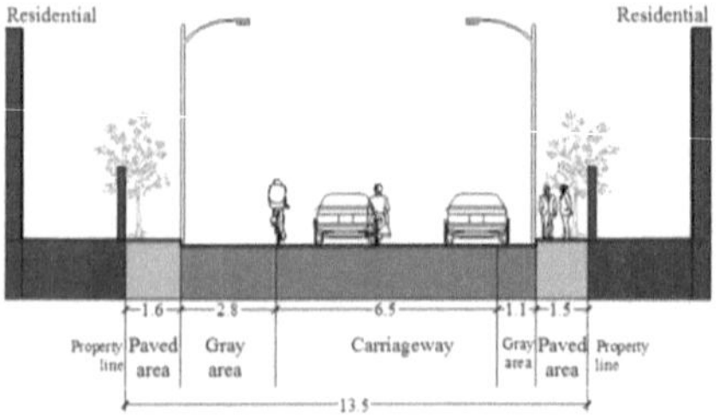

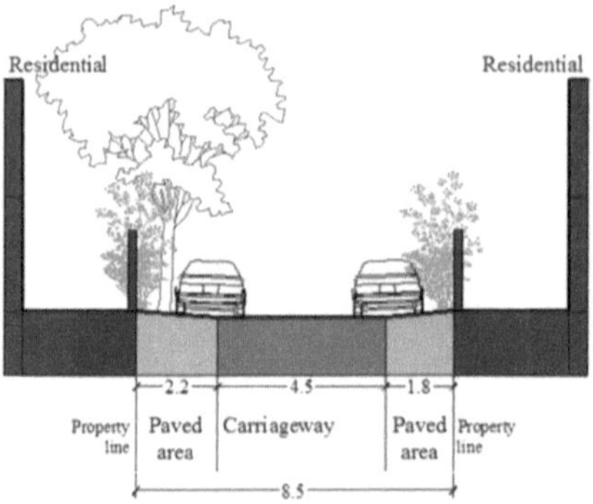

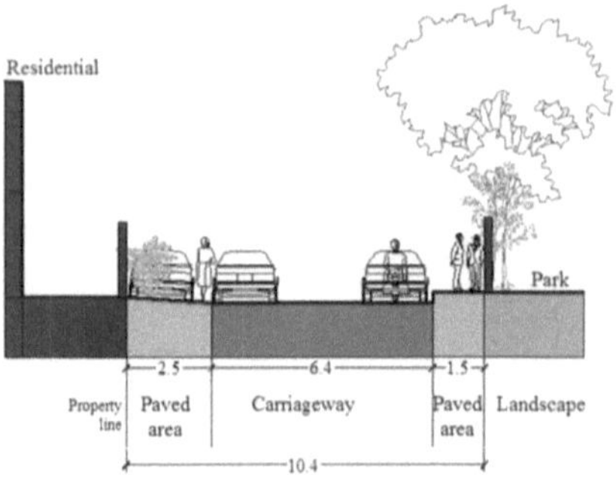

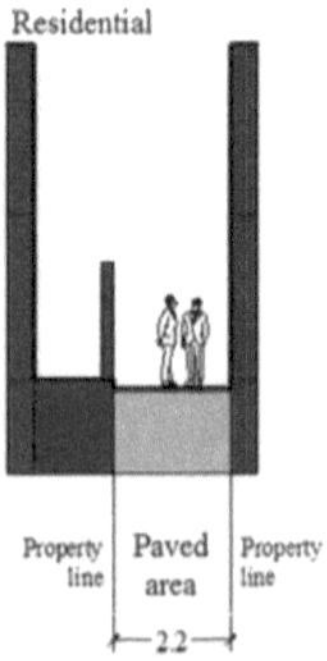

- Paved areas along both sides of carriageway but mostly encroached by parked vehicles
- Large building plots and very less visual penetration
- Very less to moderate sense of enclosure
- Intermittent shade from trees causes pedestrian discomfort in hot weather
- Intermittent sights of greenery
- Well-articulated building designs
- Parked vehicles and high vehicle speeds prohibitive for the pedestrians

Figure 4.32 Street sections and pedestrian scenario in Rani ka Bagh (N-6)

Walk Scenario in the Neighbourhoods of Amritsar City: A Case Study   **107**

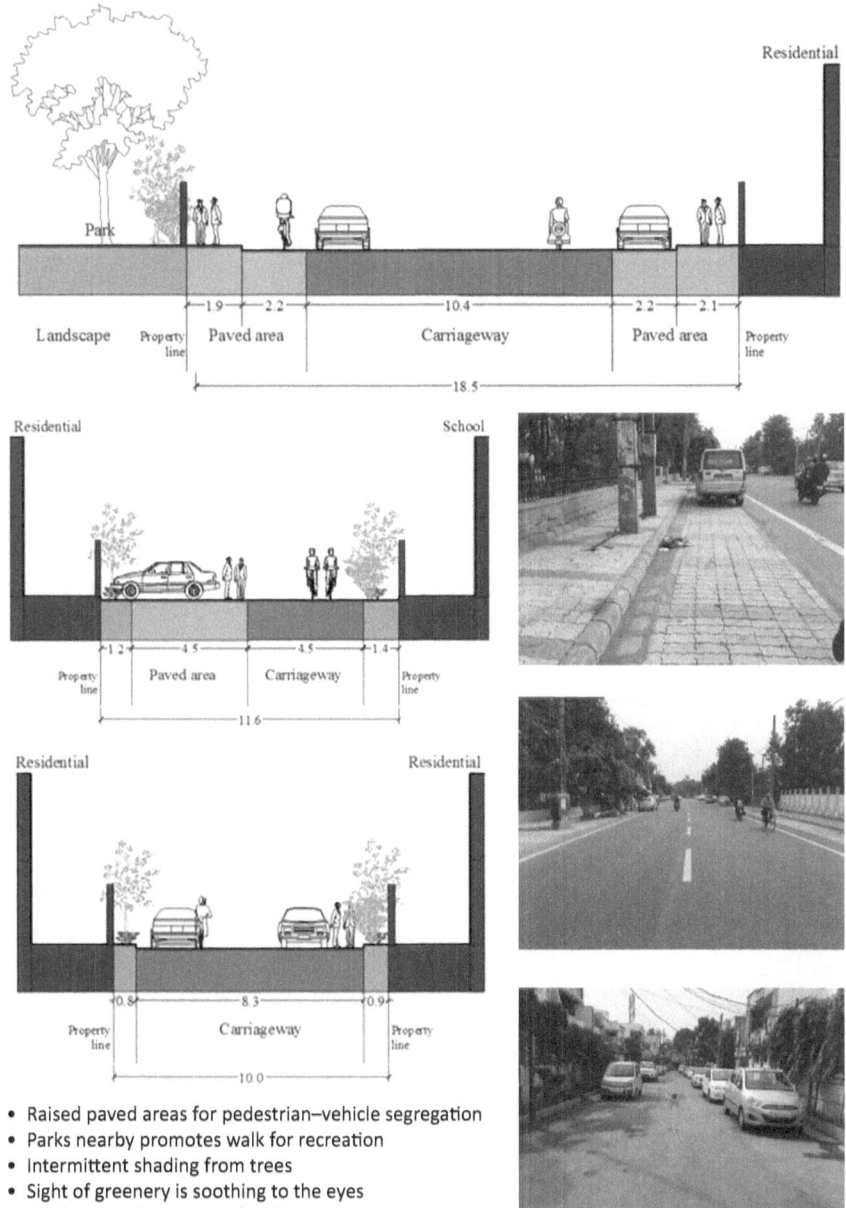

- Raised paved areas for pedestrian–vehicle segregation
- Parks nearby promotes walk for recreation
- Intermittent shading from trees
- Sight of greenery is soothing to the eyes
- Moderate to low sense of enclosure
- Well-articulated building designs
- Electricity poles, parked vehicles, etc., create obstructions
- Generally clean but pedestrian amenities grossly lacking

Figure 4.33 Street sections and pedestrian scenario in Green Avenue (N-7)

108 Towards Pedestrian-Friendly Neighbourhoods

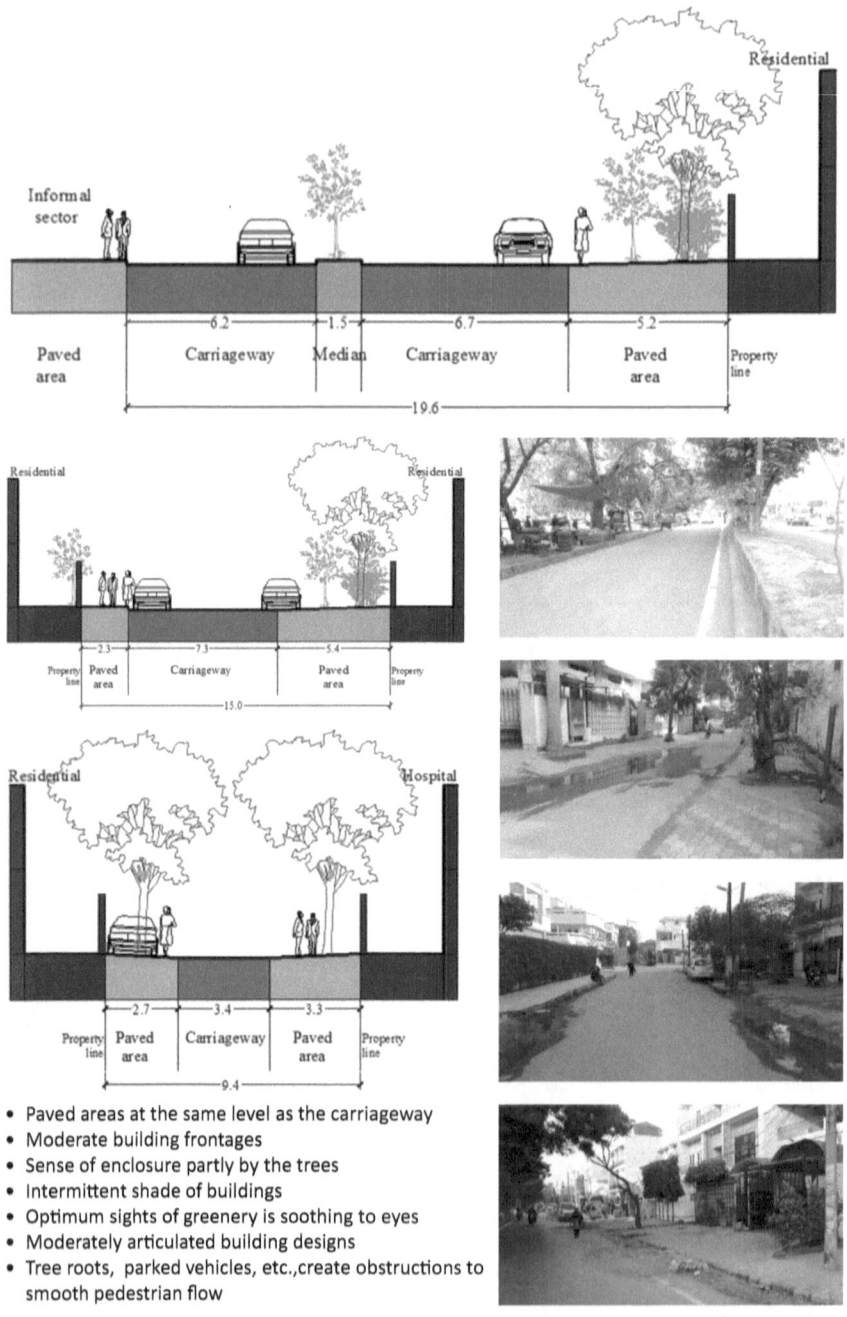

- Paved areas at the same level as the carriageway
- Moderate building frontages
- Sense of enclosure partly by the trees
- Intermittent shade of buildings
- Optimum sights of greenery is soothing to eyes
- Moderately articulated building designs
- Tree roots, parked vehicles, etc., create obstructions to smooth pedestrian flow

Figure 4.34 Street sections and pedestrian scenario in B-Block, Ranjit Avenue (N-8)

Walk Scenario in the Neighbourhoods of Amritsar City: A Case Study 109

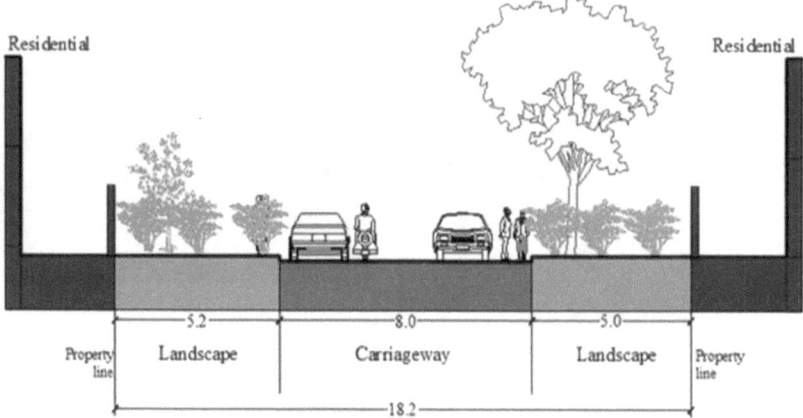

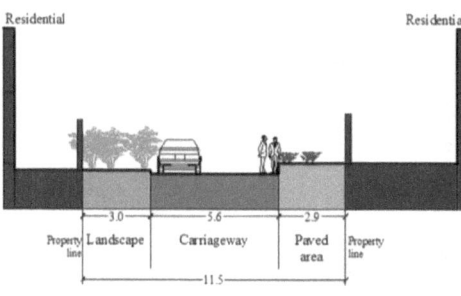

- No segregated pedestrian paths despite wide roads
- Large plot sizes
- Absolutely no sense of enclosure
- Intermittent shade of buildings
- Optimum sights of greenery
- Well-articulated building designsenthral the pedestrians
- Building projections into the public domain with pedestrians forced to walk on road
- Generally clean and visually appealing but pedestrian amenities grossly lacking

Figure 4.35 Street sections and pedestrian scenario in Defence Colony (N-9)

110 Towards Pedestrian-Friendly Neighbourhoods

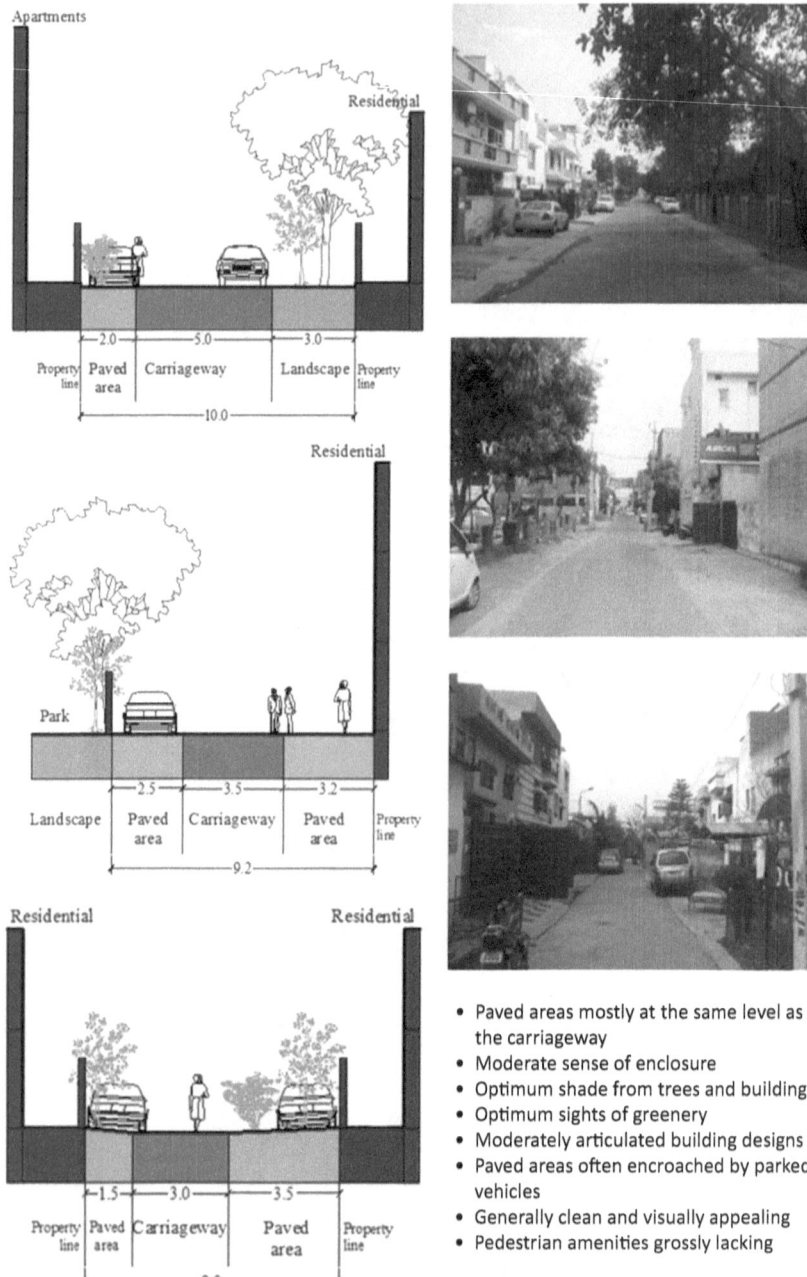

- Paved areas mostly at the same level as the carriageway
- Moderate sense of enclosure
- Optimum shade from trees and buildings
- Optimum sights of greenery
- Moderately articulated building designs
- Paved areas often encroached by parked vehicles
- Generally clean and visually appealing
- Pedestrian amenities grossly lacking

Figure 4.36 Street sections and pedestrian scenario in Housing Board Colony (N-10)

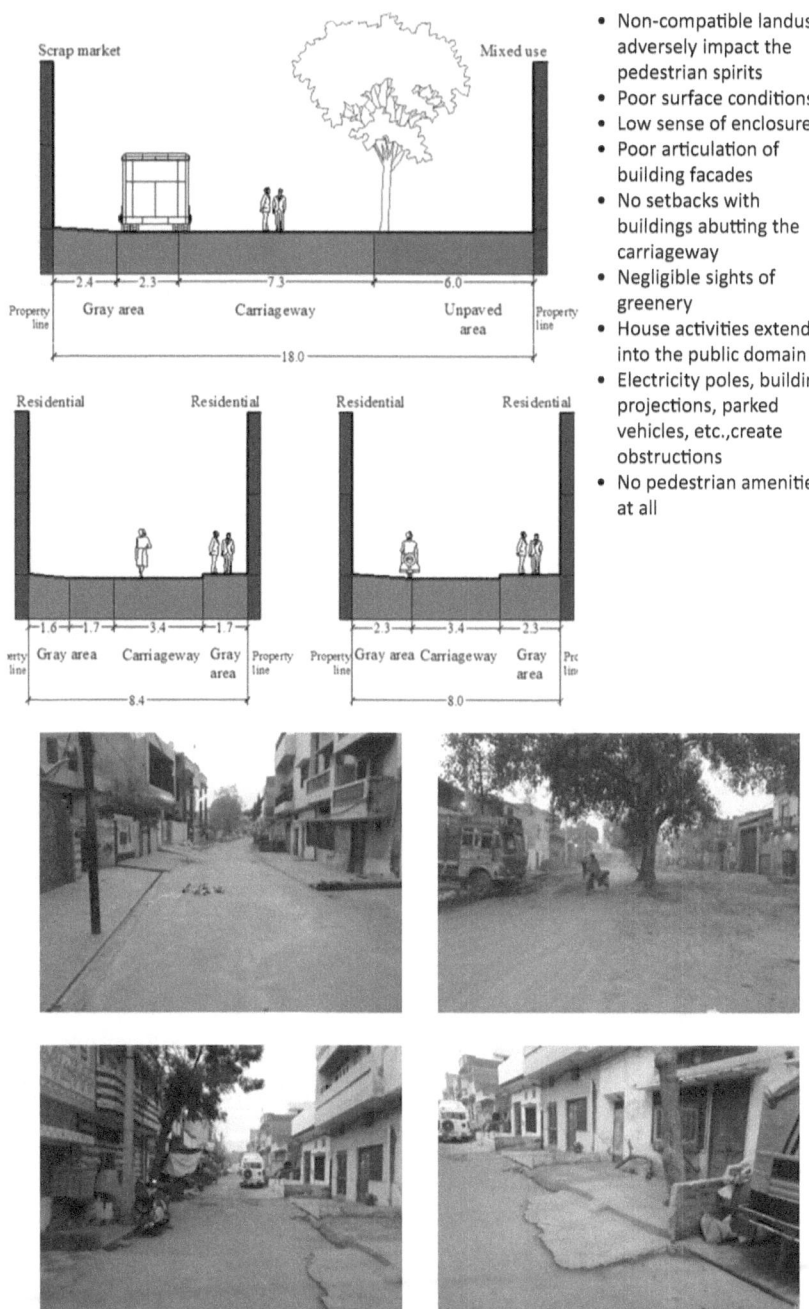

- Non-compatible landuses adversely impact the pedestrian spirits
- Poor surface conditions
- Low sense of enclosure
- Poor articulation of building facades
- No setbacks with buildings abutting the carriageway
- Negligible sights of greenery
- House activities extend into the public domain
- Electricity poles, building projections, parked vehicles, etc., create obstructions
- No pedestrian amenities at all

Figure 4.37 Street sections and pedestrian scenario in Mohan Nagar (N-11)

112 Towards Pedestrian-Friendly Neighbourhoods

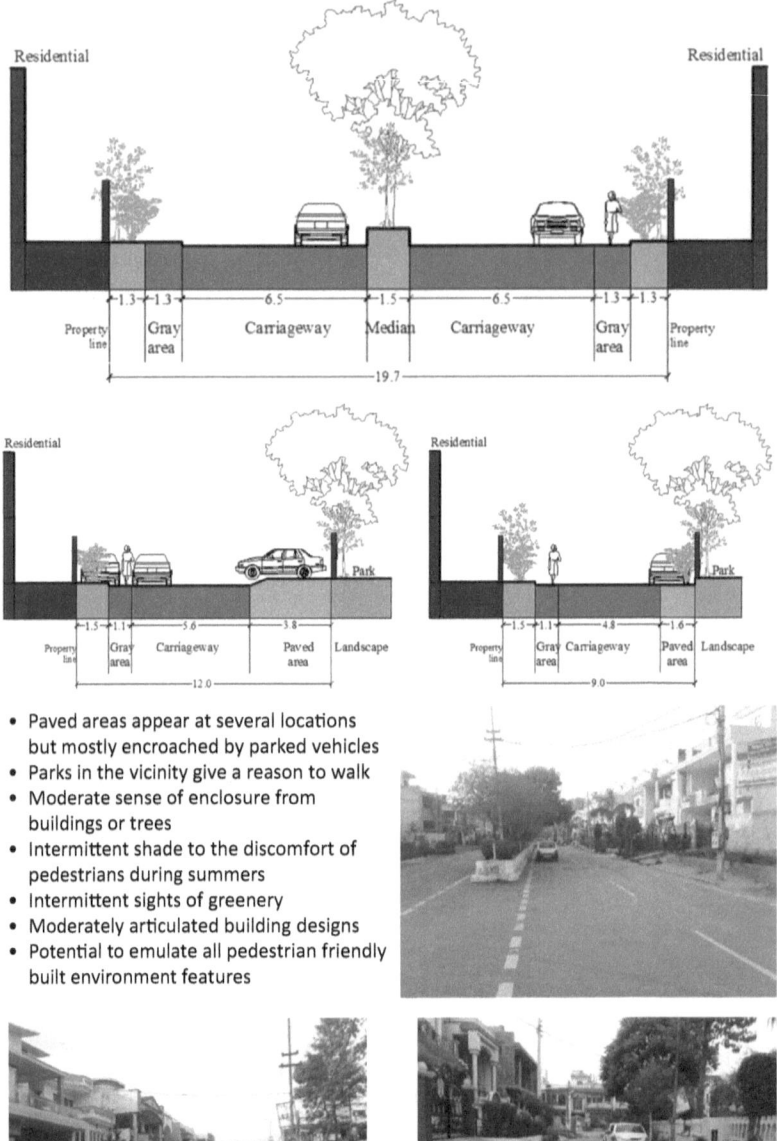

- Paved areas appear at several locations but mostly encroached by parked vehicles
- Parks in the vicinity give a reason to walk
- Moderate sense of enclosure from buildings or trees
- Intermittent shade to the discomfort of pedestrians during summers
- Intermittent sights of greenery
- Moderately articulated building designs
- Potential to emulate all pedestrian friendly built environment features

Figure 4.38 Street sections and pedestrian scenario in New Amritsar (N-12)

Walk Scenario in the Neighbourhoods of Amritsar City: A Case Study 113

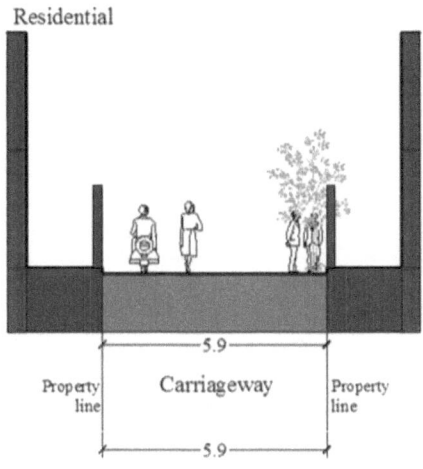

- No segregated pedestrian paths
- Narrow building frontages
- Optimumto high sense of enclosure
- Optimum shade from buildings because of narrow roads
- Absolutely no sights of greenery
- Moderately to poorly articulated building designs
- Electricity poles, building projections, etc., create obstructions
- Short entry ramps to houses encroach upon the road

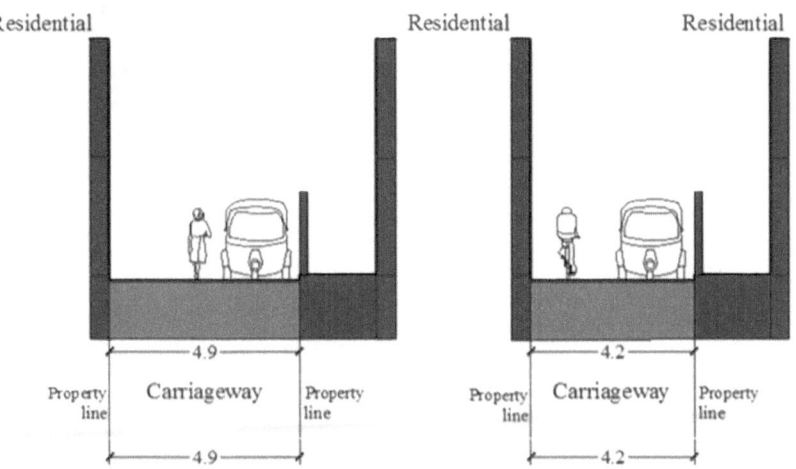

Figure 4.39 Street sections and pedestrian scenario in Bhalla Colony (N-13)

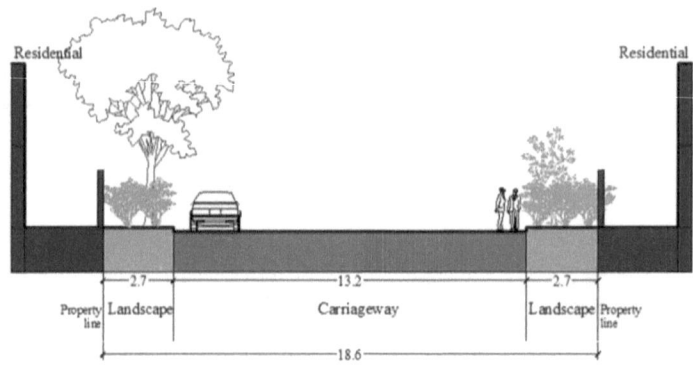

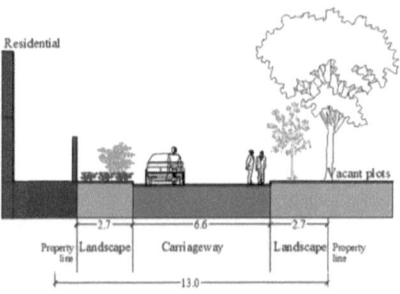

- Absolutely no segregated pedestrian paths despite large right of way
- Large plot sizes leading to longer building frontages
- Absolutely no sense of enclosure from buildings or trees
- Intermittent shade to the discomfort of pedestrians during summers
- Intermittent sights of greenery
- Well-articulated building designs add to the pedestrians' delight
- Not fully developed leaving large vacant chunks of land
- Potential to emulate all pedestrian friendly built environment features

Figure 4.40 Street sections and pedestrian scenario in Holy City (N-14)

4.4.4 Analysis of Variance of various parameters

ANOVA based on neighbourhoods: In order to find out the significance of variation in the scores for various parameters of 14 neighbourhoods, statistical analysis was performed using ANOVA. The results are indicated in Table 4.8.

Table 4.8 ANOVA based on neighbourhoods

	Parameter	Objective assessment		Subjective assessment	
		F	Sig.	F	Sig.
A	General street environment	6.015	0.000	4.344	0.000
B	Pathway availability and quality	8.817	0.000	6.682	0.000
C	Obstructions to walking	1.731	0.000	7.561	0.060
D	Traffic safety	2.444	0.000	9.442	0.005
E	Disability infrastructure			50.919	
F	Pedestrian amenities	5.361	0.000	4.105	0.000
G	Spatial quality	6.321	0.000	9.530	0.000
	Overall	5.914	0.000	12.668	0.000

It is observed that the variation is statically significant for all parameters of the segment level except subjectively assessed *obstructions to walking* parameter. *Disability infrastructure* is practically non-existent.

ANOVA based on population density categories: Further attempt was made to explore whether significant variability existed in the mean scores for three population density categories originally derived from the Master Plan document. ANOVA was conducted to investigate the 158 segments of which 101 segments represented low density neighbourhoods, 25 segments represented medium density neighbourhoods and 32 segments were from high density neighbourhoods. The post-hoc tests were undertaken to determine the direction of variability of the mean scores. The results are indicated in Table 4.9.

In case of objective assessment of parameters, it is observed that the variance in the mean scores is statistically significant for *general street environment, pathway availability and quality, obstructions to walking* and *spatial quality* as also at *overall level*. The variance is insignificant for *traffic safety* and *pedestrian amenities*. In case of subjective assessment of parameters, it is observed that the variance in the mean scores is statistically significant for all parameters except *spatial quality*.

Table 4.9 ANOVA based on population density

		Overall	Low and Medium		Low and High		Medium and High	
		Sig.	Mean Difference (L-M)	Sig.	Mean Difference (L-H)	Sig.	Mean Difference (M-H)	Sig.
Objective Assessment								
A	General street environment	0.003	−0.735	0.056	−0.832*	0.008	−0.097	0.964
B	Pathway availability and quality	0.000	3.151*	0.049	5.825*	0.000	2.673	0.205
C	Obstructions to walking	0.038	0.781*	0.049	0.421	0.302	−0.361	0.623
D	Traffic safety	0.146	0.326	0.345	0.332	0.228	0.006	1.000
E	Disability infrastructure							
F	Pedestrian amenities	0.228	0.462	0.607	−0.507	0.445	−0.969	0.210
G	Spatial quality	0.008	−0.500	0.429	−1.063*	0.007	−0.563	0.463
	Overall	0.005	3.485	0.093	4.175*	0.011	0.690	0.934
Subjective Assessment								
A	General street environment	0.002	0.388	0.136	0.584*	0.003	0.196	0.690
B	Pathway availability and quality	0.000	0.829*	0.000	0.536*	0.009	−0.293	0.462
C	Obstructions to walking	0.000	0.958*	0.000	0.293	0.131	−0.665*	0.005
D	Traffic safety	0.000	0.642*	0.002	0.529*	0.004	−0.114	0.866
E	Disability infrastructure	0.046	0.106	0.177	0.106	0.098	0.000	1.000
F	Pedestrian amenities	0.008	0.278	0.197	0.409*	0.010	0.131	0.770
G	Spatial quality	0.065	0.199	0.547	0.373	0.062	0.173	0.720
	Overall	0.000	3.400*	0.000	2.829*	0.000	−0.571	0.823

*The mean difference is significant at 0.05 level

Further investigation through the post-hoc tests reveals the significance of difference in the mean scores at 95 percent confidence level. Post-hoc tests for objective assessment reveal the following:

- For *pathway availability and quality*, significant difference in the means scores exists between low and medium density neighbourhoods and between low and high density neighbourhoods, with the low density neighbourhoods scoring better than the others.
- For the parameter *obstructions to walking*, significant difference in the mean scores is visible between low and medium density neighbourhoods, with the latter posing more obstructions to the pedestrians.
- For the parameters of *general street environment* and *spatial quality* as also at the *overall level*, significant difference in the mean scores becomes evident between low and high density neighbourhoods. While the high density neighbourhoods reflect better scores for the former two parameters, lower density neighbourhoods score better at the *overall level*.

Post-hoc tests for subjective assessment reveal the following:

- For the parameters of *pathway availability and quality* and *traffic safety* as also at the *overall level*, significant difference in the mean scores exists between low and medium density neighbourhoods, and between low and high density neighbourhoods. This generally puts low density neighbourhoods in a better perspective as compared to the rest.
- For the parameters of *general street environment* and *pedestrian amenities*, significant difference exists in the mean scores between low and high density neighbourhoods, with the former getting higher mean scores.
- For the parameter of *obstructions to walking*, there is a significant difference in the mean scores between low and medium density neighbourhoods and between medium and high density neighbourhoods with the medium density neighbourhoods scoring poorer than the other two. This seems somewhat unexpected.

The chapter at the onset premised poor walkability scenario in the neighbourhoods of Amritsar city. The low walkability scores of various neighbourhoods, with a narrow range from 32.08 to 46.59, reflect the poor responsiveness of built environment to the pedestrian context in Amritsar city.

4.5 Observations Regarding Residents' Attitudes and Perceptions

Random pedestrian surveys were conducted in the 14 neighbourhoods in order to accumulate actual sentiments of the residents, and to ensure that the recommended improvements synchronize with their expectations from the built environment. Since a small sample size was felt sufficient to elicit the requisite information within the constraints of time and resources, the survey teams were given at least 20 performas per neighbourhood. A total of 218 performas were returned by the survey teams with feedback ranging from 13 to 20 respondents per neighbourhood. The data procured from residents of diverse neighbourhoods was aggregated for the whole city. The surveyors used local language in conducting the surveys to facilitate better comprehension of the questions by the respondents.

Socio-economic profile of the respondents: The socio-economic profile of the respondents is presented through Table 4.10.

Table 4.10 Socio-economic profile of the respondents

		Frequency	Percent
1	**Gender**		
	Male	127	58.3
	Female	91	41.7
2	**Age (in years)**		
	0–30	83	38.1
	30–50	104	47.7
	>50	31	14.2
3	**Monthly household income (in rupees)**		
	< 10,000	24	11.4
	10,000–50,000	105	50.0
	50,000–2 lakhs	59	28.1
	> 2 lakhs	22	10.5
4	**Vehicle ownership**		
	Bicycles	60	27.5
	Two wheelers	173	79.4
	Car, jeep, etc.	141	64.7

It evolved from the random surveys that the majority of the survey respondents (58.3 percent) fall in the category of males. The age category of 30 to 50 years dominates (47.7 percent). As regards the monthly household income, most (50.0 percent) fall in the category of Rs. 10,000 to Rs. 50,000. Motorized vehicles are widely prevalent with two wheelers finding maximum ownership (79.4 percent) followed by cars, jeeps, etc., (64.7 percent) in various households.

Walk perception and preference of the respondents: The pedestrian respondents of the selected neighbourhoods were explored as regards their intrinsic preference for walking over driving. They were further asked how they rated pedestrian facilities in their own neighbourhoods, and whether they would like to improve their walking habits if the walkability conditions in their neighbourhoods are enhanced. The results are presented through Table 4.11.

As may be observed, 66.4 percent of the respondents prefer walking over driving either 'frequently' or 'sometimes'. As regards rating the pedestrian facilities in their respective neighbourhoods, as many as 36.7 percent of respondents consider their neighbourhoods as 'average', 29.8 percent as 'good' and 22.8 percent as 'bad'. Earlier, the field walkability surveys by trained raters had generated an average walkability score of 40.09 for the segment level parameters in the neighbourhoods of Amritsar city with maximum and minimum values being 46.59 and 32.08, respectively. The results seem skewed towards 'average' in both cases.

Table 4.11 Walk perception and preferences of the respondents

		Frequency	Percent
5	How often do you prefer walking over driving?		
	Almost every time	19	8.8
	Frequently	72	33.2
	Sometimes	72	33.2
	Very few times	43	19.8
	Never	11	5.1
6	How do you rate the pedestrian facilities in your locality?		
	Very Good	6	2.8
	Good	65	29.8

Contd...

Contd...

		Frequency	Percent
	Average	80	36.7
	Bad	50	22.9
	Very Bad	17	7.8
7	**If walkability conditions are enhanced, would you like to improve your walking habits?**		
	Certainly	106	48.6
	May think	89	40.8
	Not at all	12	5.5
	Don't know	11	5.0

The results further show that the neighbourhood residents are not contented and would like to have improvement in their pedestrian environment for enhancing their walking habits. As many as 48.6 percent feel 'certain' and 40.8 percent feel that they 'may think' about improving their walking habits if walkability conditions are improved. The results are fairly encouraging since undertaking planning and design endeavour for the pedestrians seems relevant.

Chi-square tests to measure association: An attempt was made to find out whether responses to the three questions posed to the survey participants had some association with population density of neighbourhoods, gender, age or monthly household income. Chi-square test was performed to study this association. The results are depicted in Table 4.12.

Table 4.12 Chi-square tests to measure association

		Population density	Gender	Age	Monthly household income
How often do you prefer walking over driving?	χ^2 value	12.493	5.133	7.528	18.946
	Asymp. Sig. (2-sided)	0.131	0.274	0.481	0.090
How do you rate the pedestrian facilities in your locality?	χ^2 value	17.580	4.080	8.471	9.353
	Asymp. Sig. (2-sided)	0.025	0.395	0.389	0.673
If walkability conditions are enhanced, would you like to improve your walking habits?	χ^2 value	4.272	1.566	6.533	18.712
	Asymp. Sig. (2-sided)	0.640	0.667	0.366	0.028

Chi-square test revealed a significant association of responses of 'How do you rate the pedestrian facilities in your locality?' with population density. The question 'If walkability conditions are enhanced, would you like to improve your walking habits?' found significant association with monthly household income. In order to further explore the degree of association of responses in the above two categories, crosstab analysis was undertaken.

The responses to the question 'How do you rate the pedestrian facilities in your locality?' were explored as regards its degree of association with the population density categories. The responses were received from 136 residents of low density neighbourhoods, 33 residents of medium density neighbourhoods and 49 residents of high density neighbourhoods. The results are indicated in the Table 4.13.

Table 4.13 Crosstab Test to measure the Degree of Association with population density

			Population density			Total
			Low	Medium	High	
How do you rate the pedestrian facilities in your locality?	Very good	Count	6	0	0	6
		Percent*	100.0	0.0	0.0	100.0
		Percent**	4.4	0.0	0.0	2.8
	Good	Count	51	4	10	65
		Percent*	78.5	6.2	15.4	100.0
		Percent**	37.5	12.1	20.4	29.8
	Average	Count	45	16	19	80
		Percent*	56.3	20.0	23.8	100.0
		Percent**	33.1	48.5	38.8	36.7
	Bad	Count	25	9	16	50
		Percent*	50.0	18.0	32.0	100.0
		Percent**	18.4	27.3	32.7	22.9
	Very bad	Count	9	4	4	17
		Percent*	52.9	23.5	23.5	100.0
		Percent**	6.6	12.1	8.2	7.8
	Total	Count	136	33	49	218
		Percent*	62.4	15.1	22.5	100.0
		Percent**	100.0	100.0	100.0	100.0

Percent* – percent within "How do you rate the pedestrian facilities in your locality?"
Percent** – percent within "Population Density"

As may be observed, categories of 'very good' and 'good' received 41.9 percent of responses from 'low population density' category, 12.1

percent of responses from 'medium population density' category and 20.4 percent of responses from 'high population density' category. 48.5 percent of the respondents from 'medium population density' category rate the pedestrian facilities in their respective neighbourhoods as 'average'; while 40.9 percent of the respondents from 'high population density' category rate the pedestrian facilities in their respective neighbourhoods as 'bad to very bad'. It is observed that the neighbourhoods with low population densities are rated better from pedestrian perspective. This seems quite contrary to the claims of several scholars who propagate higher densities for promoting walkability.

The responses to the question 'If walkability conditions are enhanced, would you like to improve your walking habits?' were explored as regards its degree of association with monthly household income. The responses were received from 24 residents of 'less than 10,000' category, 105 residents of '10,000 to 50,000' category, 59 residents of '50,000 to 2 lakhs' category and 22 residents of 'more than 2 lakhs' category. The results are indicated in Table 4.14.

Table 4.14 Crosstab Test to measure the Degree of Association with monthly household income

			Monthly household income (in rupees)				
			Less than 10,000	10,000 to 50,000	50,000 to 2 lakhs	More than 2 lakhs	Total
If walkability conditions are enhanced, would you like to improve your walking habits?	Certainly	Count	16	54	20	9	99
		Percent*	16.2	54.5	20.2	9.1	100.0
		Percent**	66.7	51.4	33.9	40.9	47.1
	May think	Count	7	41	33	7	88
		Percent*	8.0	46.6	37.5	8.0	100.0
		Percent**	29.2	39.0	55.9	31.8	41.9
	Not at all	Count	1	5	4	2	12
		Percent*	8.3	41.7	33.3	16.7	100.0
		Percent**	4.2	4.8	6.8	9.1	5.7
	Don't know	Count	0	5	2	4	11
		Percent*	0.0	45.5	18.2	36.4	100.0
		Percent**	0.0	4.8	3.4	18.2	5.2
	Total	Count	24	105	59	22	210
		Percent*	11.4	50.0	28.1	10.5	100.0
		Per cent**	100.0	100.0	100.0	100.0	100.0

Percent* – percent within "If walkability conditions are enhanced, would you like to improve your walking habits?"
Percent** – percent within "Monthly household income (in rupees)"

As may be observed, categories of 'certainly' and 'may think' received 95.9 percent of responses from 'less than 10,000' category, 90.4 percent of responses from '10,000 to 50,000' category, 89.8 percent of responses from '50,000 to 2 lakhs' category and 72.7 percent of responses from 'more than 2 lakhs' category. This shows that the lesser income people are more enthusiastic on having an enhanced pedestrian-responsive neighbourhood built environment. In the absence of sufficient income, they become captive users to the roads or streets as pedestrians. Overall percentage of 89.0 percent in the categories of 'certainly' and 'may think' are positive signs that justify the endeavour to address pedestrian issues in the neighbourhoods of Amritsar.

Preference of the respondents as regards desired improvements in pedestrian environment: The resident respondents were further explored about the specific improvements they would like to have in the neighbourhood built environment. Based on literature, ten possible desired improvements were identified for the neighbourhoods of Amritsar city. The 218 respondents were asked to rank these from 1st to 10th based on their priority for specific improvements desired from pedestrian environment. Feedback sought from the residents would signify a wider social acceptability for the improvements recommended to enhance the pedestrian environment in the neighbourhoods of Amritsar city.

Alfonzo et al. (2008) postulated four pedestrian expectations in this regard, namely, accessibility, safety and security, comfort and attractiveness or pleasurability. Each of the ten options offered to the respondents pertained to one or more of these expectations (Table 4.15). However, accessibility that forms the basic criteria for a person's decision to walk, being a neighbourhood level parameter, shall become relevant in the planning of new neighbourhoods.

Table 4.15 List of desired improvements in the pedestrian environment

Codes	Desired improvements	Relevant pedestrian expectations
DI-1	Exclusive pathways for pedestrians	Safety
DI-2	More shade along the pathway (from buildings/ trees)	Comfort
DI-3	Reduced and slow traffic on road	Safety
DI-4	Clean and litter free pathways	Attractiveness

Contd...

Contd...

Codes	Desired improvements	Relevant pedestrian expectations
DI-5	Remove obstacles and/or parking from footpaths	Safety
DI-6	Improve surface conditions (remove potholes, etc.)	Safety
DI-7	Provide/ improve amenities (benches, drinking fountains, etc.)	Comfort
DI-8	Easy access for the physically or visually disabled	Safety
DI-9	Make the streets more attractive visually	Attractiveness
DI-10	Improved street lighting	Comfort

The rankings provided by the 218 resident respondents to the desired improvements are compiled in Table 4.16, and the weighted averages for each of the desired improvements were calculated as under:

$$(WA_i) = \frac{(\Sigma R_i \times N_i)}{\Sigma N_i}$$

where WA represents the weighted average for the desired improvement, R represents the allocated score for a particular rank and N represents the number of respondents. The score allocated for 1st rank is 10, 2nd rank is 9 and so on up to 10th rank with score of 1.

Table 4.16 Residents' rankings and weighted averages for desired improvements

Ranks	No. of respondents in each rank category										Weighted averages for desired improvements
Codes for desired improvements	1st	2nd	3rd	4th	5th	6th	7th	8th	9th	10th	
DI-1	75	31	14	10	5	30	14	16	16	7	7.04
DI-2	64	38	24	16	8	39	16	4	5	4	7.43
DI-3	10	24	20	25	23	24	22	35	11	24	5.27
DI-4	24	46	33	19	19	27	20	13	5	12	6.61
DI-5	5	10	28	33	21	21	44	28	15	13	5.18
DI-6	9	15	14	19	29	14	18	26	37	37	4.47
DI-7	23	18	17	25	23	19	11	22	37	23	5.24
DI-8	8	19	5	11	38	6	14	15	39	63	3.98
DI-9	0	7	25	31	25	17	26	28	42	17	4.61
DI-10	0	10	38	29	27	21	33	31	11	18	5.18

Walk Scenario in the Neighbourhoods of Amritsar City: A Case Study

From section 4.5.2, it follows that the different density zones in the city would require varied treatments for enhancing their walkability. Therefore, desired improvements were also analysed independently for the three identified density zones. The results are presented in Table 4.17 and Figure 4.41.

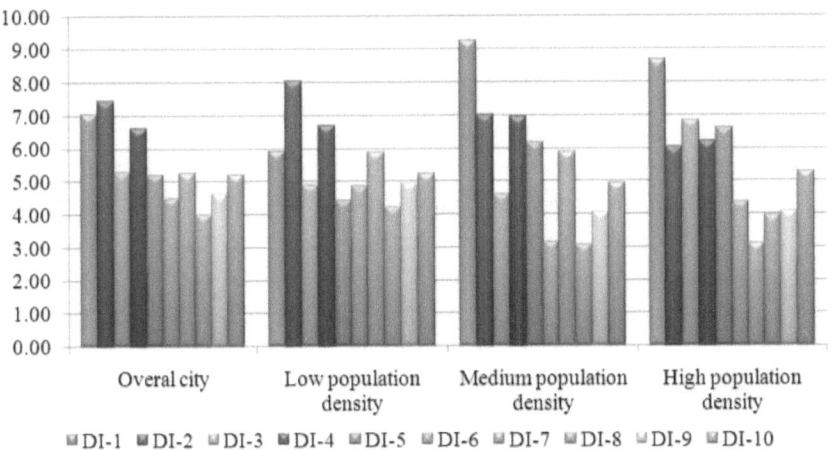

Figure 4.41 Desired improvements based on population density

Table 4.17 Weighted averages for desired improvements based on population density

	Overall city	Low population density	Medium population density	High population density
DI-1	7.04	5.91	9.24	8.67
DI-2	7.43	8.04	7.00	6.02
DI-3	5.27	4.87	4.58	6.84
DI-4	6.61	6.68	6.94	6.18
DI-5	5.18	4.43	6.18	6.59
DI-6	4.47	4.84	3.15	4.35
DI-7	5.24	5.87	5.88	3.08
DI-8	3.98	4.22	3.06	3.94
DI-9	4.61	4.94	4.03	4.06
DI-10	5.18	5.21	4.94	5.27

The parameter DI-2 representing the *residents desire for more shade along the pathway (from buildings/ trees)* gets the highest value at the overall city level as also in the low population density neighbourhoods. This shows that comfort reigns supreme in the pedestrians' desires. However, this desire takes a back-seat in the medium and high density neighbourhoods. The dense built fabric of the walled city area to some extent justifies this. Medium and high density neighbourhoods exhibit top most desire for *exclusive pathways for pedestrians (DI-1)*, the desire that is not echoed equally in the low density neighbourhoods. *Easy access for the physically or visually disabled (DI-8)* is one of the least valued in all density zones. High population density neighbourhoods are also deterred by the traffic and desire to *reduced and slow traffic on road (DI-3)*, while the low density neighbourhoods feel more concerned about the attractiveness aspect reflected by second highest average score for *clean and litter free pathways (DI-4)*.

The chi-square test had earlier revealed significant association of monthly household income to the desire to improve walking habits, with the lesser income people seemingly more enthusiastic on having an enhanced pedestrian-responsive neighbourhood built environment. Therefore, the variability of desired improvements was questioned based on income categories as well. The weighted averages for desired improvements are indicated in Table 4.18 and Figure 4.42 based on monthly household incomes of the respondents.

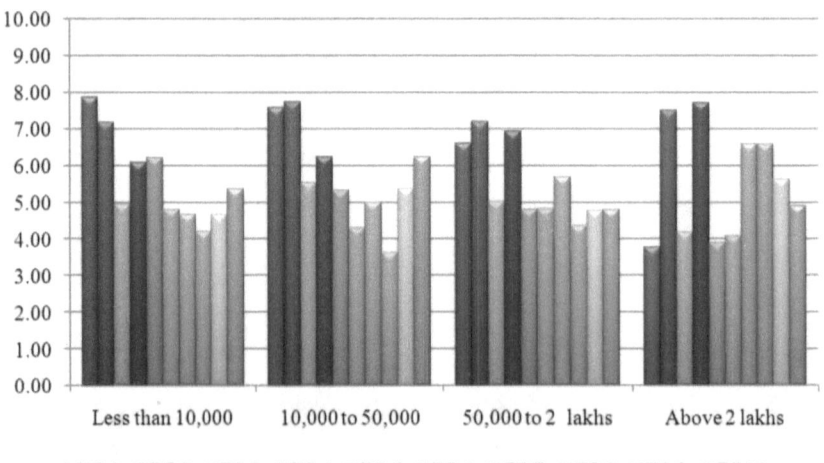

Figure 4.42 Desired improvements based on monthly household income

It is observed that the desire for *more shade along the pathway (from buildings/ trees) (DI-2)* is consistent across all the income categories. The desire for *exclusive pathways for pedestrians (DI-1)* is very strong except in case of highest income category, that values *clean and litter free pathways (DI-4)* much more than others. This category also seems more sensitive to the needs of the physically challenged depicted in the weighted average of 6.59 for *easy access for the physically or visually disabled (D-8)*.

Table 4.18 Weighted averages for desired improvements based on monthly household income

	Less than 10,000	10,000 to 50,000	50,000 to 2 lakhs	Above 2 lakhs
DI-1	7.88	7.59	6.61	3.77
DI-2	7.17	7.75	7.20	7.50
DI-3	4.96	5.55	5.02	4.18
DI-4	6.08	6.25	6.93	7.73
DI-5	6.21	5.32	4.80	3.91
DI-6	4.79	4.30	4.81	4.09
DI-7	4.67	4.99	5.69	6.59
DI-8	4.21	3.63	4.36	6.59
DI-9	4.67	5.36	4.78	5.64
DI-10	5.38	6.25	4.80	4.91

4.6 Findings for walk scenario in the neighbourhoods of Amritsar city

The findings bring forth the deficiencies that shall form the premise for recommending and injecting pedestrian-oriented improvements into the neighbourhood built environment.

(1) *Neighbourhood streets of Amritsar are deficient in most walkability related features*: The analysis of 158 randomly selected street segments of 14 neighbourhoods of Amritsar city builds up a scenario for the entirety of street networks in the city. The study observed that only 22.2% of the streets are provided with sidewalks that in 62.5% of the cases are intermittent. Parked vehicles form the most prominent obstructions to walking followed -by poles, mesh of wires, etc., and prevail along 73.4% and 60.1% of the streets, respectively. It was strange to find that traffic didn't seem

to be much of an issue with as many as 48.7% of the streets that faced medium traffic conditions. But considering the fact that traffic and parked vehicles are factors that show large variations on hourly basis, therefore, more rigorous analysis of these attributes shall provide a truthful status. Going by the rising vehicular ownership trends, these are bound to create impediments to smooth pedestrian flow therefore need to be addressed. Speed bumps seemed to be the only traffic-calming devices utilised but only on 36.1% of the neighbourhood streets. Zebra crossings were found on a mere 3.8% of the streets. There is a complete neglect for the pedestrian amenities and disability infrastructure. Further, the shade whether from buildings or trees too was mostly intermittent (54.4%). The subjective assessment based on various parameters too placed most of the segments in bad to very bad categories with trifling responses in good to very good categories.

(2) *Spatial quality in Amritsar neighbourhoods is somewhat favourable*: It is observed that all the attributes of spatial quality have most prevalence in the moderate category. It is to be noted that certain attributes of spatial quality were required to be subjectively assessed. As many as 54.4% of the streets offer some sense of enclosure due to buildings or trees to the pedestrians; 58.2% of the streets have some articulation in building designs; 51.9% of the streets have moderate level of visual penetrability at ground floor level; and 51.3% of the streets offered moderate level of greenery intermittently placed. Subjective assessment on a 5-point Likert Scale too found spatial quality to be average in 47.5% cases.

(3) *Walkability audits by trained personnel may well replace subjective feedback from residents in the future studies*: Many studies in the past have attempted to measure walkability through subjective feedback from the residents implying huge costs and time implications. Further, replicating similar efforts for another location would always be tedious. The present study found the assessment of the street segments through walkability audit to be in sync with the residents' expectations. This shows that in future studies, the walkability audit by trained personnel may well provide

a comprehensive overview of the walkability scenario so as to form a basis for recommending improvements in the existing setup.

References

Clifton, K., Ewing, R., Knaap, G. J., and Song, Y. (2008). Quantitative analysis of urban form: A multidisciplinary review. *Journal of Urbanism: International Research on Place making and Urban Sustainability* 1(1): 17–45.

Clifton, K. J., Livi Smith, A. D., and Rodriguez, D. (2007). The development and testing of an audit for the pedestrian environment. *Landscape and Urban Planning* 80(1-2): 95–110.

CSE (2009). *Footfalls: Obstacle Course to Livable Cities.* Centre for Science and Environment, Delhi. < http://www.cseindia.org/userfiles/walkability_pdf.pdf >

McMillan, T. E., Cubbin, C., Parmenter, B., Medina, A. V., and Lee, R. E. (2010). Neighbourhood sampling: How many streets must an auditor walk? *The International Journal of Behavioural Nutrition and Physical Activity* 7(20).

MoUD (2008). *Study on Traffic and Transportation Policies and Strategies in Urban Areas in India.* Prepared by Wilbur Smith Associates for the Ministry of Urban Development, Government of India, New Delhi.

Moudon, A. V., and Lee, C. (2003). Walking and bicycling: An evaluation of environmental audit instruments. *American Journal of Health Promotion* 18(1): 21–37.

Parks, J. R., and Schofer, J. L. (2006). Characterizing neighbourhood pedestrian environments with secondary data. Transportation Research Part D: *Transport and Environment* 11(4): 250–263.

PMIDC (2012). *Comprehensive Mobility Plan for Various Cities of Punjab State (Package – I) Amritsar City.* Punjab Municipal Infrastructure Development Company, Department of local Government Punjab. Draft Final Report.

Rundle, A. G., Bader, M. D. M., Richards, C. A., Neckerman, K. M., and Teitler, J. O. (2011). Using Google street view to audit neighbourhood environments. *American Journal of Preventive Medicine* 40(1): 94–100.

SAI Consulting Engineers (2010). *Draft Master Plan of Amritsar (2010-31)*, Punjab Urban Planning and Development Authority, Mohali.

Sallis, J. F. (2009). Measuring physical activity environments: A brief history. *American Journal of Preventive Medicine* 36(4Suppl): S86–S92.

Singhal, M. (2018a). Auditing and scoring the pedestrian micro-environments of varied neighbourhoods in Amritsar city. *Urban India* 38(I): 28–45.

Singhal, M. (2018b). Assessment of neighbourhood walkability: issues and approaches. *Nagarlok* XLX (1), 25–41.

Singhal, M. (2018c). Walkability perception and pedestrian expectations: Seeking residents' feedback regarding neighbourhood environments of Amritsar city. *Nagarlok* L (3), 40–55.

Su, M., Du, Y., Liu, Q., Ren, Y., Kawachi, I., Lv, J., and Li, L. (2014). Objective assessment of urban built environment related to physical activity--development, reliability and validity of the China Urban Built Environment Scan Tool (CUBEST). *BMC Public Health* 14(1): 109.

Tiwari, G. (2001). Pedestrian infrastructure in the city transport system: A case study of Delhi. *World Transport Policy & Practice* 7(4), 13–18.

5
The Way Forward

Indian cities have traditionally remained pedestrian-friendly. However, with the motorized transport grabbing the centre-stage, pedestrian interests have been badly bruised. Now with the ill-effects of increased mobility getting visible and the wisdom of walking getting rediscovered, it is time to radically change the whole focus of transport and urban policies from vehicle-centric to people-centric in the utilization of our urban environment. Enough knowledge in this regard is readily available awaiting implementation in the Indian context. Amritsar city, by utilising the prevalent knowledge for emulating the spirit of pedestrian-friendly neighbourhoods, may pave the way for a large number of Indian cities having similar built environments. This chapter, therefore, first offers elaborate recommendations for practical application of pedestrian-oriented principles in the neighbourhoods of Amritsar city; and then goes about making general recommendations for stimulating pedestrian-friendly neighbourhood environment in the Indian cities.

5.1 Application of Pedestrian-Friendly Principles in the Neighbourhoods of Amritsar City

Based on a rigorous investigation of Amritsar city, Chapter 4 concludes that the pedestrians are very poorly addressed in the planning and design of its neighbourhoods. The information generated out of this book provides a framework for decision making, and has an immediate practical application. To begin with, the 14 selected neighbourhoods may be immediately upgraded from pedestrian perspective to serve as a prototype to propagate the spirit of walking at local level. In this context, the following actions are recommended:

- Complete absence of exclusive pedestrian domain is starkly visible in the surveys. Therefore, as the first step, pathways need to be developed along all segments in all neighbourhoods. While in medium and low density neighbourhoods, they may appear as sidewalks; in the dense areas like walled city, this would require strategies for complete denial of certain street stretches to the motorists on one hand, and re-routing vehicles and identifying parking locations on the other. Thus, walkability implies that the various modes as also pedestrians must co-exist along most streets; barring the very narrow streets of highly dense neighbourhoods where the only solution shall be absolutely demeaning the vehicles. Though it may sound theoretically simple and easy, it shall be immensely difficult in most cases to vacate part of the roadway for creating pathways.
- Thermal comfort is an important issue in medium and low density neighbourhoods, which suggests large scale plantation of shade-giving trees.
- The importance of pedestrian amenities and disability infrastructure cannot be undermined. Pedestrian amenities shall comprise benches/seats, trash bins, street vending, socialising space, drinking water, kiosks and signage. 'Guidelines for pedestrian facilities' as enshrined in the IRC code 103:2012 would come handy in this regard (refer Section 3.1.3).

In order to achieve immediate execution of the actions recommended above by the concerned authorities, templates have been developed for the various road widths (Figures 5.1 to 5.4). Thus, a single set of standards, determined by the road widths, shall be suitable across all the neighbourhoods of Amritsar city irrespective of their location, size and typology. These templates demonstrate the following features:

- Pedestrian paths may be provided along one side for road widths of 7.5–9.0 meters and along both sides for wider roads.
- Footpaths, as mentioned in Figure 3.1, to have three distinct zones: dead width of 0.5 meters to accommodate any building projections, planting beds, creepers, etc.; clear pedestrian zone of minimum 1.8 meters width; planting/fixture zone of minimum 1.7–2.0 meters width accommodating tree pits, parking, fixtures, utilities and access ramps. The latter two zones may be reduced to 1.5 meters and 1.0 meter respectively in case of 7.5 meters wide roads.
- Kerb height of 100–150 mm (refer Figure 3.2) may be provided. Kerb ramps (refer Figures 3.3 and 3.4) and pedestrian crossings (zebra or table top) at junctions shall enhance accessibility.
- Safety bollards (refer Figure 3.9) may be utilised to prevent U-turning of vehicles along wider roads. Tighter corner radius (refer Figure 2.11) shall check upon the turning speeds in the residential areas.

While the above recommendations are implemented, innovative ways of traffic calming (refer Figures 2.13a/b) may also be introduced in certain existing and upcoming neighbourhoods, thus exemplifying complete streets instilled with a sense of place. The enhancement of the neighbourhood environments from pedestrian perspective may serve as an inspiration for other cities to replicate, thus injecting the spirit of walking in the daily lives of all.

Walk-related research has to a large extent remained theoretical only. It is time to move towards implementation so that real-time benefits derived out of the enhanced neighbourhood environment may be studied, quantified and compared. However, implementation in the existing neighbourhoods may not be easy because of the limitations of street width, general non-willingness of car users to transform themselves for the sake of pedestrian environment and several other factors. In this context, meticulous planning followed by strict implementation would have to be ensured by the concerned agencies.

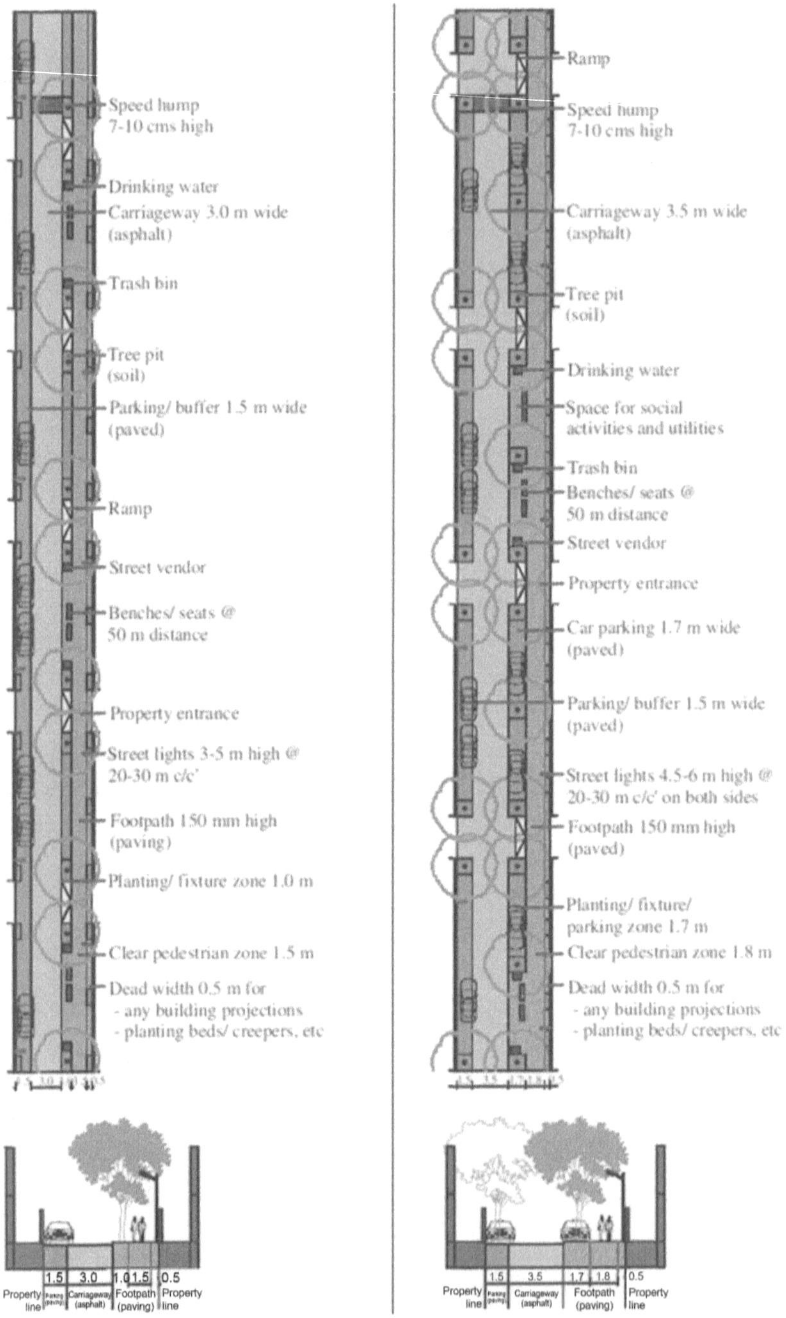

Figure 5.1 Proposed layout for 7.5 m and 9 m wide streets in Amritsar city

The Way Forward **135**

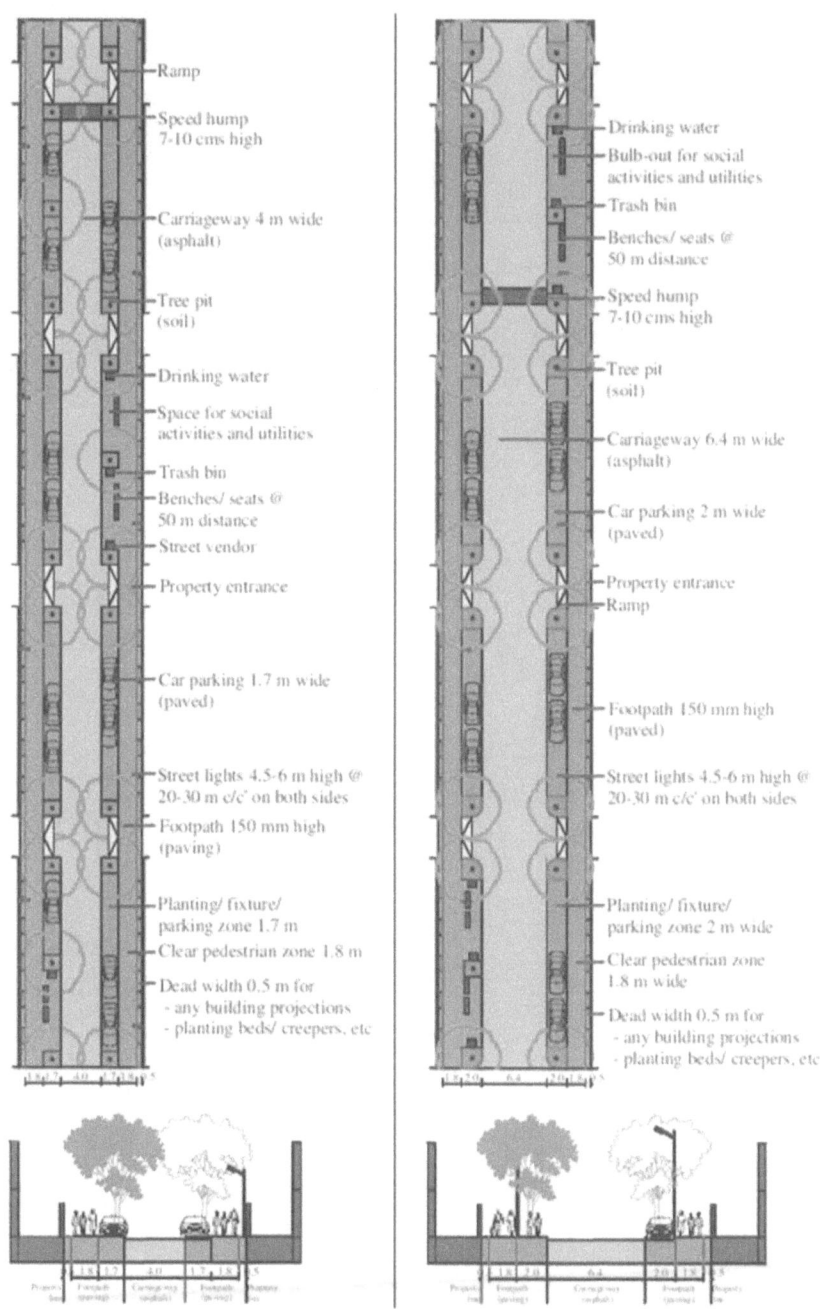

Figure 5.2 Proposed layout for 12 m and 15 m wide streets in Amritsar city

136 Towards Pedestrian-Friendly Neighbourhoods

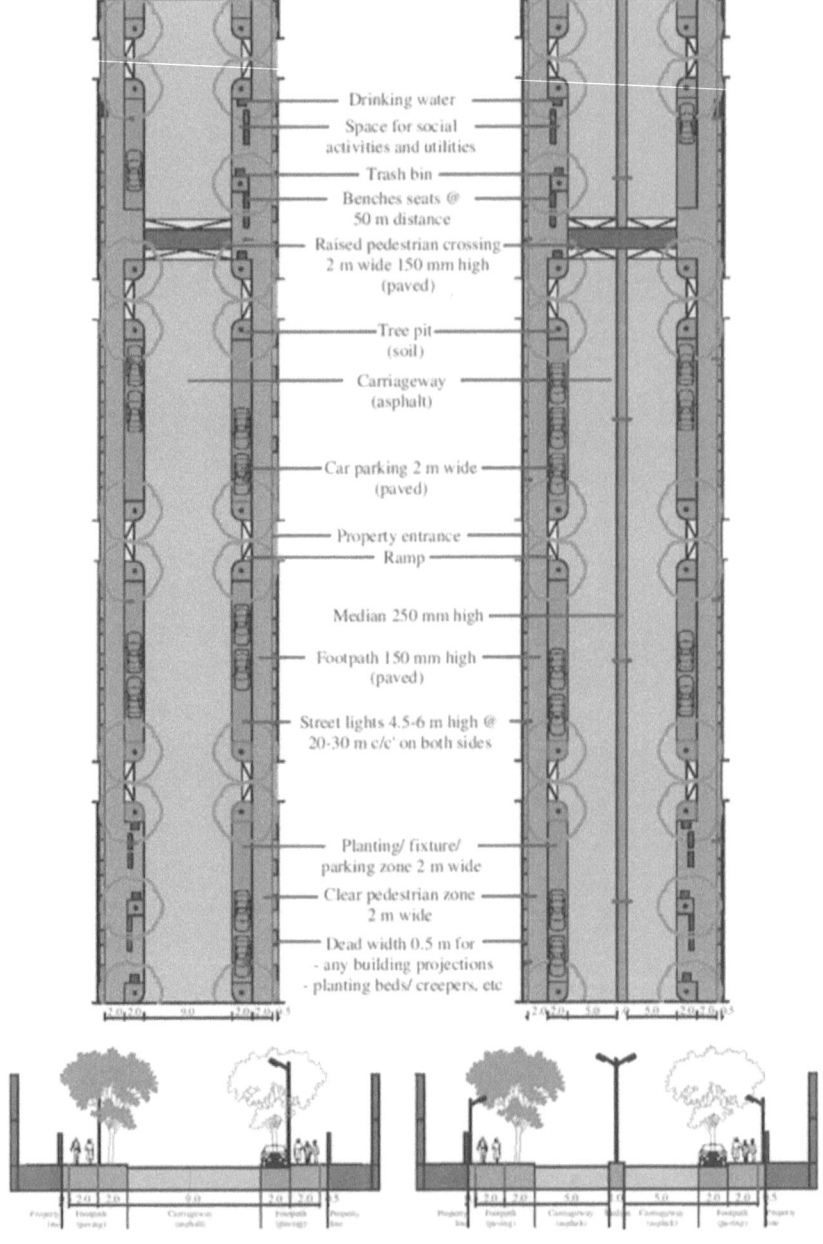

Figure 5.3 Proposed layout for 18 m and 20 m wide streets in Amritsar city

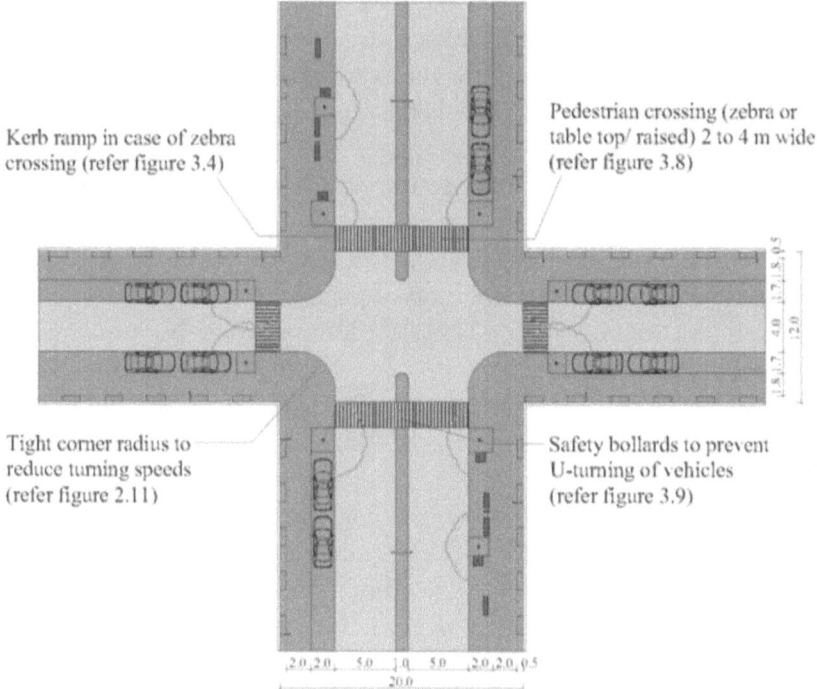

Figure 5.4 Proposed layout at the road intersections

5.2 Recommendations for Pedestrian-Friendly Neighbourhood Environment in the Indian Cities

Findings of the rigorous investigation of neighbourhood-built environments of Amritsar city from pedestrian perspective entails a strong message for all Indian cities: "Our neighbourhood built environment needs to be modulated to respond to the pedestrians' imminent needs and desires, namely, *accessibility, safety and security, comfort* and *attractiveness or pleasurability*". Having realised this, the need is to

- Take up rigorous investigation of neighbourhoods in various cities in order to bring forth their specific issues related to the built environment in addition to the general concerns of all Indian cities. The Pedestrian Environmental Data Scan (PEDS), the audit instrument initially developed by the University of

Maryland and University of North Carolina, USA, and further customized to suit the Indian conditions (Annexure II), may be utilised in its entirety for the exploration.
- In innumerable cases whereby pedestrian scenario is similar to Amritsar city, the templates for Amritsar city, developed specifically for the neighbourhood environments, may serve as a ready-reckoner, deserving of immediate practical application.

It must be realised that the development of templates is just one step forward. Successful implementation of plan proposals shall be highly a daunting task requiring various stakeholders to contribute their pie at different points of time.

- The Central Government plays its role by way of administering relevant policies. In this regard, NUTP 2006 clearly acknowledges the need of exclusive pedestrian lanes, better pavement facilities and amenities. However, the concern remains mostly for the high traffic corridors. The requirement of exclusive space for pedestrians must percolate down more emphatically to the neighbourhood or area level so as to reinstall walking as a way of life amongst all income categories. Pedestrian plans must be made mandatory and conditional to any sort of infrastructure funding.
- The national policy links monetary support with the formulation and implementation of 'specific area plans in congested urban areas' and generally hints at 'appropriate changes in bye-laws and legislation to free the public carriage way from parked vehicles in the residential areas'. As per Constitution of India, urban development and hence urban transport is the responsibility of state government. The state through its urban development authorities and the department of transport must take relevant initiatives, while utilising the provisions enshrined in the NUTP 2006, to improve the pedestrian scenario in the urban neighbourhoods. The national policy itself must become more explicit in this regard.
- The municipalities shall be the key stakeholders for pedestrian-facility development, implementation as also its maintenance in the neighbourhoods. While intensive campaigns for spreading public awareness and seeking citizen cooperation shall be essential,

strict implementation of relevant rules and regulations shall have to be ensured through suitable fines and other punishments. The municipalities must devise a funding mechanism that will ensure a regular flow of money for the successful accomplishment of this task.
- While the private sector is generally required to comply with the policies and regulations set by the government, it must consciously and truthfully consider and prioritize pedestrian access and movement in all sorts of land development endeavours.
- There are certain non-governmental organisations dedicated to the cause of promoting walk culture in the Indian cities. While their initiatives are laudable, they may extend their role in promoting improvements of pedestrian facilities in the neighbourhoods of Indian cities. At the city level, more such dedicated institutions with sufficient resources must emerge in order to ensure that policies and projects are properly implemented.
- Citizens must themselves be aware and demand mechanisms that shall promote the green travel habits while minimising the negative impacts of vehicular traffic. All design guidelines and regulations would be futile unless backed by the support of the civic society.

Thus the various stakeholders must converge and play their identified roles in most efficient manner for the ultimate purpose of improving walkability and pedestrian facilities in the neighbourhoods of Indian cities.

Bibliography

- Aggarwal, A. Samarthayam (2009). *Guidelines for inclusive pedestrian facilities*. Report for IRC, TRIPP, IIT Delhi, BRT Design Specifications.
- Alfonzo, M., Boarnet, M. G., Day, K., Mcmillan, T., and Anderson, C. L. (2008). The relationship of neighbourhood built environment features and adult parents' walking. *Journal of Urban Design* 13(1): 29–51.
- Anderson, S. (1978). *On Streets*. Edited for The Institute for Architecture and Urban Studies. MIT Press, Cambridge.
- Appleyard, D. (1981). *Livable Streets*. University of California Press, Los Angeles, California.
- Bhardwaj, P. (2010). *The Pedestrian and the Road*. Working Paper Series. Centre for Public Policy Research, Kerala. < http:// www.cppr.in >
- CAI-Asia (2011). *Walkability in Indian cities*. Clean Air Initiative for Asian Cities (CAI-Asia) Center and Shakti Sustainable Energy Foundation. Pasig City, Philippines.
- CAI-Asia and SSEF (2012). *Improving Footpaths in Indian Cities through Walkability Surveys and Tighter Policies*. Clean Air Initiative for Asian Cities (CAI-Asia) Center and Shakti Sustainable Energy Foundation. Pasig City, Philippines.
- Clifton, K. J., Livi Smith, A. D., and Rodriguez, D. (2007). The development and testing of an audit for the pedestrian environment. *Landscape and Urban Planning* 80(1–2): 95–110.
- Clifton, K., Ewing, R., Knaap, G. J., and Song, Y. (2008). Quantitative analysis of urban form: a multidisciplinary review.

Journal of Urbanism: International Research on Place making and Urban Sustainability 1(1): 17–45.

- CSE (2009). *Footfalls: Obstacle Course to Livable Cities.* Centre for Science and Environment, Delhi. < http://www.cseindia.org/userfiles/walkability_pdf.pdf >
- Department for Transport (2007). *Manual for Streets.* Thomas Telford Publishing, London, UK.
- EPC (2013). *Sustainable Urban Transport Principles and Implementation Guidelines for Indian Cities.* Environmental Planning Collaborative, Ahmedabad, India.
- Ewing, R. (2000). *Pedestrian and Transit-Friendly Design: A Primer for Smart Growth.* EPA Smart Growth Network, ICMA, Washington, DC. < http://www.epa.gov/dced/pdf/ptfd_primer.pdf >
- Ewing, R., and Handy, S. (2009). Measuring the unmeasurable: Urban design qualities related to walkability, *Journal of Urban Design* 14(1): 65–84.
- Gallion, A. B., and Eisner, S. (eds.) (1984). *The Urban Pattern: City Planning and Design.* CBS Publishers, Delhi. pp. 223–226.
- GDOT (2003). *Pedestrian and Streetscape Guide.* Georgia Department of Transportation. Otak, Inc.
- Goodman, R., and Tolley, R. (2003). The decline of everyday walking in the UK: Explanations and policy implications. *Sustainable Transport: Planning for Walking and Cycling in Urban Environments.* Rodney Tolley (ed). Woodland Publishing Limited, England.
- Horn, A. (2004). Reflections on the concept and conceptualization of the urban neighborhood in societies in transition: The case of Pretoria (South Africa). *Dela*, Vol. 21, pp. 329–340.
- IRC (1989). Guidelines for Pedestrian Facilities. Indian Roads Congress. IRC: 103-1988.
- IRC (2012). *Guidelines for Pedestrian Facilities (First Revision).* Indian Roads Congress. IRC: 103-2012.
- Jacobs, A. B. (1995) *Great Streets.* MIT Press, Cambridge, Massachusetts.

- Jacobs, J. (1992). *The Death and Life of Great American Cities*. Random House Inc., United States.
- Jani, A., and Kost, C. (2013). *Footpath design - A guide to creating footpaths that are safe, comfortable, and easy to use*. Prepared for Institute for Transportation and Development Policy. www.itdp.org
- Kost, C., and Nohn, M. (2011). *Better Streets, Better Cities – A Guide to Street Design in Urban India*. Institute for Transportation and Development Policy (ITDP) and Environmental Planning Collaborative (EPC). http://www.itdp.org/ betterstreets
- Lynch, K. (1984). Good City Form. The MIT Press, England. pp. 400–402.
- Mehta, V. (2008). Walkable streets: pedestrian behavior, perceptions and attitudes. *Journal of Urbanism: International Research on Placemaking and Urban Sustainability* 1(3): 217–245.
- MAoG (2005). *Pedestrian Policies and Design Guidelines*. Maricopa Association of Governments.
- McMillan, T.E., Cubbin, C., Parmenter, B., Medina, A.V. and Lee, R.E. (2010). Neighbourhood sampling: how many streets must an auditor walk? *The International Journal of Behavioural Nutrition and Physical Activity* 7(20).
- MoRTH (2013). *Road Transport Year Book (2011-12)*. Ministry of Road Transport & Highways, Government of India, New Delhi.
- MoUD (2006). *National Urban Transport Policy*. Ministry of Urban Development, Government of India, New Delhi.
- MoUD (2008). *Study on Traffic and Transportation Policies and Strategies in Urban Areas in India*. Prepared by Wilbur Smith Associates for the Ministry of Urban Development, Government of India, New Delhi.
- MoUD (2013). *Code of Practice for Design of Urban Roads*. Prepared by the Transportation Research and Injury Prevention Programme (TRIPP) for the Institute of Urban Transport (IUT), Ministry of Urban Development, Government of India.
- Moudon, A. V. (ed). (1987). *Public Streets for Public Use*. Van Nostrand Reinhold, New York.

- Moudon, A. V., and Lee, C. (2003). *Walking and bicycling: an evaluation of environmental audit instruments.* American Journal of Health Promotion 18(1): 21-37.
- NTDPC (2014). *India Transport Report: Moving India to 2032.* National Transport Development Policy Committee. Published on behalf of Planning Commission, GOI. Routledge - Taylor and Francis Group, New Delhi.
- NZ Transport Agency (2008). *Pedestrian Planning and Design Guide.* New Zealand.
- Parks, J. R., and Schofer, J. L. (2006). Characterizing neighbourhood pedestrian environments with secondary data. Transportation Research Part D: *Transport and Environment* 11(4): 250-263.
- PMIDC (2012). *Comprehensive Mobility Plan for Various Cities of Punjab State (Package – I) Amritsar City.* Punjab Municipal Infrastructure Development Company, Department of local Government Punjab. Draft Final Report.
- Rundle, A. G., Bader, M. D. M., Richards, C. A., Neckerman, K. M., and Teitler, J. O. (2011). Using Google street view to audit neighbourhood environments. *American Journal of Preventive Medicine* 40(1): 94-100.
- SAI Consulting Engineers (2010). *Draft Master Plan of Amritsar (2010-31),* Punjab Urban Planning and Development Authority, Mohali.
- Sallis, J. F. (2009). Measuring physical activity environments: A brief history. *American Journal of Preventive Medicine* 36(4Suppl): S86-S92.
- SANDAG (2002). *Planning and Designing for Pedestrians: Model Guidelines for the San Diego's Region.* San Diego's Regional Planning Agency. <http://www.sandag.org/uploads/publicationid/publicationid_713_3269.pdf>
- SFPD (2010). *San Francisco Better Streets Plan - Policies and Guidelines for the Pedestrian Realm.* San Francisco Planning Department. <http://www.sfbetterstreets.org>
- Singh, S. K. (2005). Review of urban transportation in India. *Journal of Public Transportation* 8(1): 79-97.

- Su, M., Du, Y., Liu, Q., Ren, Y., Kawachi, I., Lv, J., and Li, L. (2014). Objective assessment of urban built environment related to physical activity--development, reliability and validity of the China Urban Built Environment Scan Tool (CUBEST). *BMC Public Health* **14**(1): 109.
- Singhal, M. (2017). *Pedestrian Oriented Planning and Design of Neighbourhoods: Measuring and Evaluating the Walkability of Diverse Neighbourhoods in Amritsar City.* Unpublished PhD research submitted to GNDU, Amritsar.
- Talen, E. (2002). Pedestrian access as a measure of urban quality. *Planning Practice and Research* **17**(3): 257–278.
- TfL (2004). *Making London a Walkable City - The Walking Plan for London.* Transport for London. < http://www.tfl.gov.uk >
- Tibbalds, F. (2005). *Making People-Friendly Towns: Improving the Public Environment in Towns and Cities.* Spon Press, London and New York.
- Tiwari, G. (2001). Pedestrian infrastructure in the city transport system: A case study of Delhi. *World Transport Policy & Practice* **7**(4): 13-18.
- Tolley, R. (ed) (2003). *Sustainable transport: Planning for walking and cycling in urban environments*, Woodhead Publishing Limited, Cambridge, England.
- UTTIPEC (2010). *Street Design Guidelines.* Unified Traffic and Transportation Infrastructure (Planning and Engineering) Centre, DDA, New Delhi. < http://uttipec.nic.in/writereaddata/linkimages/7554441800.pdf >
- Walters, D., and Brown, L. L. (2004). *Design First: Design-based Planning for Communities.* Architectural Press, Amsterdam.
- Wheeler, S. M. (2013). *Planning for sustainability: Creating livable, equitable and ecological communities.* Routledge, London and New York.
- WSDT (1997). *Pedestrian Facilities Guidebook - Incorporating Pedestrians into Washington's Transportation System.* Washington State Department of Transportation.
- Whittick, A. (ed.) (1974). *Encyclopedia of Urban Planning.* McGraw-Hill Book Company, USA. pp. 714–715.

- Yeang, L. D. et al. (2007). *Manual for Streets.* Produced by a team of consultants on behalf of the Department for Transport, and Communities and Local Government. Thomas Telford Publishing, London.

Websites
- https://en.wikipedia.org/wiki/Compact_city
- https://en.wikipedia.org/wiki/New_Urbanism
- https://en.wikipedia.org/wiki/Transit-oriented_development
- https://everipedia.org/wiki/New_pedestrianism/

Annexures

Annexure I: Pedestrian Environmental Data Scan (PEDS) Audit Tool

Name : _____ Date : _____ Study Area : _____
Segment number : _____ Time : _____ Weather : _____

SUBJECTIVE ASSESSMENT: Segment…
Enter 1,2,3 or 4 for 1 = Strongly Agree, 2 = Agree, 3 = Disagree, 4 = Strongly Agree
……..is attractive for walking _____ 1
……..is attractive for cycling _____ 2
……..feels safe for walking _____ 3
……..feels safe for cycling _____ 4

0. SEGMENT TYPE
Low volume road _____ 1
High volume road _____ 2
Bike or ped path – skip section C _____ 3

A. ENVIRONMENT
1. Uses in Segment *(all that apply)*
Housing – Single Family Detached _____ 1
Housing – Multi Family _____ 2
Housing – Mobile Homes _____ 3
Office/ Institutional _____ 4
Restaurant/Café/Commercial _____ 5
Industrial _____ 7
Vacant/Undeveloped _____ 8
Recreation _____ 9
2. Slope
Flat _____ 1
Slight hill _____ 2
Steep hill _____ 3
3. Cul-de-sac/Dead-end
Segment has dead end _____ 1
Segment continues _____ 2
Road dead ends but path continues _____ 3

B. PEDESTRIAN FACILITY *(skip if not present)*
4. Type(s) of pedestrian facility *(all that apply)*
Footpath (worn dirt path) _____ 1
Paved trail _____ 2
Sidewalk _____ 3
Pedestrian street (closed to cars) _____ 4
Rest of the questions in section B refer to the best pedestrian facility selected above.
5. Path material (all that apply)
Asphalt _____ 1
Concrete _____ 2
Paving bricks or flag stone _____ 3
Gravel _____ 4
Dirt or sand _____ 5
6. Path obstructions *(all that apply)*
Poles or signs _____ 1
Parked cars _____ 2
Trees _____ 3
Garbage cans _____ 4
Other _____ 5
7. Buffers between road and path *(all that apply)*
Hard buffer
Fence _____ 1
Trees _____ 2
Hedges _____ 3
Soft buffer
Landscape _____ 1
Grass _____ 2
Path distance from curb (feet) _____ 3
Path width (feet) _____ 4

If no sidewalk, skip now to section C
8. Sidewalk completeness/continuity
Sidewalk is complete _____ 1
Sidewalk is incomplete _____ 2
9. Sidewalk connectivity to other sidewalks/ crosswalks
Number of connections _____ 1
10. Sidewalk condition/maintenance
Poor (many bumps/cracks/holes) _____ 1
Fair (some bumps/cracks/holes) _____ 2
Good (very few bumps/cracks/holes) _____ 3
Under repair _____ 4

C. ROAD ATTRIBUTES *(skip if path only)*
11. Condition of road
Poor (many bumps/cracks/holes) _____ 1
Fair (some bumps/cracks/holes) _____ 2
Good (very few bumps/cracks/holes) _____ 3
Under repair _____ 4
12. Number of lanes
# of lanes to cross _____ 1
13. Posted speed limit
None posted _____ 1
(mph) _____ 2
14. On-street parking *(if pavement is unmarked, check only if cars parked)*
Parallel or diagonal _____ 1
Go to Q 17 - None _____ 2
15. Off-street parking lot spaces
0-5 _____ 16-25 _____ 25+ _____
If none, go to Q 17
16. Must you walk through a parking lot to get to most buildings?
Yes _____ 1
No _____ 2
17. Driveways
There are driveways in segment _____ 1
There are no driveways in segment _____ 2
18. Traffic control devices *(all that apply)*
Traffic light _____ 1
Stop sign _____ 2
Traffic circle _____ 3
Speed bumps _____ 4
Chicanes or chokers _____ 5
19. Curb-cuts in segment
Yes _____ 1
No _____ 2
20. Crossing aids in segment *(all that apply)*
Cars must stop
Pavement markings _____ 1
Yield to pedestrian paddles _____ 2
Pedestrian signal _____ 3
Crossing aids
Median/traffic island _____ 1
Curb extension _____ 2
Overpass/underpass _____ 3
Warning to cars
Pedestrian crossing street sign _____ 1
Flashing warning _____ 2

D. WALKING/CYCLING ENVIRONMENT
21. Lighting
None _____ 1
Poor _____ 2
Fair _____ 3
Good _____ 4
22. Amenities
Garbage cans _____ 1
Benches _____ 2
Water fountain _____ 3
Bicycle parking _____ 4
Street vendors/vending machines _____ 5
23. Are there way-finding aids?
No _____ 1
Yes _____ 2
24. Number of trees shading walking area
None or very few _____ 1
Some _____ 2
Many/dense _____ 3
25. Degree of enclosure
Little or no enclosure _____ 1
Some enclosure _____ 2
Highly enclosed _____ 3
26. Power lines along segment?
No _____ 1
Low voltage/distribution line _____ 2
27. Cleanliness (Is there litter, garbage, broken glass or graffiti?)
+None or almost none _____ 1
Yes some _____ 2
Yes lots _____ 3
28. Articulation in building designs
Little or no articulation _____ 1
Some articulation _____ 2
Highly articulated _____ 3
29. Building setbacks from street
At edge of sidewalk _____ 1
Within 20 feet of sidewalk _____ 2
More than 20 feet from sidewalk _____ 3
30. Bicycle lane
None or not marked _____ 1
Striped bicycle lane _____ 2
31. Transit facilities
No _____ 1
Yes _____ 2

Source: Clifton et al., 2007

Annexure II: Parameters and Attributes of Walkability Survey

I. **General Street Environment**

General street environment captures the basic character of the street that triggers walking behaviour. The following four related walkability attributes were explored:

1. *Street hierarchy* distinguishes the streets into three categories: access street, collector street and arterial/sub-arterial road. Access streets provide access to bordering properties and areas. Majority of trips in urban areas usually originate or terminate on these streets. Collector streets distribute the traffic from access streets to arterial and sub-arterial roads. They are characterized equally by mobility and access, and carry moderate traffic volumes. Arterial and sub-arterials are the primary city roads characterized by high mobility, large traffic volumes and restricted access from carriageway to the sides. The survey audited all the streets simultaneously for both sides except in case of the sub-arterials or arterials.

2. *Types of buildings or land uses* identify the variety of uses that the various plots of land or buildings were put to: mixed use, residential flatted, residential plotted, recreational (park/playground), office or commercial, institutional, workshops or garages or industrial, vacant or undeveloped lot. As it emerges out of literature review, certain uses enhance walkability while the others have a dampening effect. The survey counted only those uses that were directly accessible from the segment. Abandoned buildings were counted under their intended uses.

3. *Average building/ plot frontage* considers street part of the building and is categorized as narrow (< 6.0 m), moderate (6.0–9.0 m) or wide (> 9.0 m).

4. *Segment connectivity* refers to the number of street connections irrespective of segment length, and is categorized as more than six, four to six and less than four.

II. **Pathway Availability and Quality**

These reflect the need for exclusive pedestrian movement spaces while also ensuring quality. They form the basic element needed to entice people to walk. The following attributes pertain to this parameter:

5. *Type of pedestrian path* considers whether the street is fully pedestrianised and is closed to cars or there is a sidewalk or worn dirt footpath running along the road. In case of the former, the next three attributes shall become irrelevant.
6. *Path location* identifies the distance of the path from the road kerb in three categories: more than 1.0 m, within 1.0 m or just next to it. Distance from the road kerb creates buffer where larger shady trees and other landscaping may be accommodated.
7. *Path width* is categorized as more than 1.8 m, from 1.2 m to 1.8 m or less than 1.2 m. Wider paths can accommodate higher volume of pedestrians and more room for amenities. Where path width varied, the average or typical values were considered.
8. *Kerb type* may be categorized as mountable, non-mountable or no kerb. The kerb type was assessed based on the ease with which it was mountable using a bicycle.
9. *Path material* is distinguished as precast pavers or stone paving, concrete or brick paving or gravel, dirt or sand. While precast or stone pavers are often decorative and enhance the pedestrian experience, dirt or sand paths seem inhospitable.
10. *Path condition* based on the degree of existence of any bumps or cracks or potholes or weeds categorizes the paths as good, moderate, poor or under repair.
11. *Path continuity* considers availability of mostly continuous or intermittent paths. Intermittent paths create discomfort and rule out the complete pedestrian experience.

III. Obstructions to Walking

Obstructions impede pedestrian movement and cause inconvenience. For the able-bodied, they create a situation where they have to walk out into the street or the buffer area to get around them. They become even more of a nuisance for the disabled who cannot easily manoeuvre around the obstructions. The obstructions whether permanent or temporary reduce the effective width of the street. Surface conditions endanger pedestrian safety. The indicators of walk obstructions are:

12. *Permanent obstructions* account for any or all of the obstructions that are permanent in nature such as poles, mesh of wires, signage, public art, bus shelters, garbage bins or heaps, benches, trees, shrubs, bushes, open gutters or building projections.

13. *Temporary obstructions* account for any or all of the obstructions that are temporary in nature such as street hawkers or vendors, parked vehicles, portable signs or furniture or shop stands.
14. *On-street parking scenario* captures level of nuisance created by parked vehicles in three categories: on-street parking not allowed, moderate number of parked vehicles with maximum 1/3rd street façade as a rough indicator or the domination of parked vehicles.
15. *Surface condition or maintenance* based on the degree of existence of any bumps or cracks or potholes or weeds categorizes the streets as good, moderate, poor or under repair.

IV. Traffic Safety

This refers to the ease with which pedestrians cross roads without exposure to vehicles, the indicators being the following:

16. *Traffic volume* considers degree of traffic conditions hampering pedestrian movement and is categorized as low to very low, medium or high.
17. *Posted speed limit* identifies whether there is any signboard cautioning the vehicles, and is categorized as up to 30 kmph, more than 30 kmph or none posted.
18. *Number of traffic lanes* capture the vulnerability of pedestrians while crossing streets or roads and are categorized as 1 to 2 lanes, 3 to 4 lanes or more than 4 lanes. While the streets with two or less lanes represent pedestrian-friendly streets, more lanes are usually found among streets with higher traffic volume and are uninviting to pedestrians.
19. *Crossing aids* consider the various aids that facilitate pedestrians while crossing the roads such as zebra crossing, median refuge or traffic island or kerb extension or pedestrian signals. Median islands provide pedestrians with a safe refuge in case of wide roadways that are difficult to traverse in a single traffic cycle. Kerb extensions at intersections narrow down the traffic lanes reducing pedestrian-crossing distances and calming the traffic.
20. *Traffic-calming devices* identify the mechanism for slowing the vehicles for the benefit of the pedestrians such as traffic lights, stop signs or bollards, traffic circle or roundabout, speed bumps, chicanes or chokers. Only those traffic-calming devices were

counted that were located within the segment, not those that were visible but located outside the segment.

V. Disability Infrastructure
This investigated the built environment for its sensitivity to the accessibility needs of the visually or physically disabled or hearing impaired.
21. *Any accessibility features* such as kerb ramps, tactile surfaces or auditory signals shall be recorded.

VI. Pedestrian Amenities
Pedestrian amenities provide comfort and convenience, thereby enhancing walking experience. Walkability indicators related to pedestrian amenities are:
22. *Availability of pedestrian amenities* considers the availability of as many such amenities: garbage bins, street furniture, drinking fountains, public toilets, bus stop/ shelter or street vendors.
23. *Condition of pedestrian amenities* considers the maintenance part of the existing amenity as to whether it is properly working or is not maintained or in working state.
24. *Location of pedestrian amenities* questions whether these are located in an exclusive fixture (or planting) zone along the pathway or are impediments to pedestrian movement.
25. *Signage and public art* are categorized as provided and appropriately located, provided but ill maintained and at inappropriate location, or not provided at all.
26. *Overall cleanliness/ maintenance* based on the degree of existence of any litter, rubbish, graffiti, etc. distinguishes streets as good, fair or poor. Leaves, branches, bushes, litter or broken glass, etc., all count towards cleanliness based on the amount and visibility in the pedestrian path.
27. *Street lighting* is expected to light up the pedestrian realm and is categorized as pedestrian scale, road oriented or none available. Pedestrian scale lighting fixtures illuminate the pedestrian path in an aesthetically pleasing manner. Road-oriented lighting and lighting from nearby buildings can incidentally illuminate the pedestrian path, but their main purpose is to illuminate the road or building features.

28. *Availability of shade* considers the shade either from trees or buildings in a continuous or intermittent manner or the complete lack of it.

VII. Spatial Quality

The spatial quality considers the volumetric expanse of streets that stimulates our senses, and is described by the following attributes:

29. *Building setbacks from sidewalk/ road edge* considers whether these abut the sidewalks or are within 6 m or are set farther than that. Buildings at the edge of the sidewalk are the most accessible.
30. *Building heights* are categorized as 1 to 2 storeyed, 3 to 4 storeyed or more than that. Building heights may be estimated by counting the rows of windows on the building. If the segment has more than one type of building height, the most prominent type is selected. Taller buildings indicate density and provide enclosure.
31. *Degree of enclosure* considers the enclosure formed by the buildings or trees and is understood as highly enclosed, some enclosure or little to no enclosure. A street would be highly enclosed if the buildings lining the street are within 10 feet of the sidewalk and there is a cross-sectional design ratio of approximately one (height) to two (width), or less. If the view is partially enclosed, but there is still some wide-open spaces then it would have some enclosure. If there is mostly empty space within the pedestrian's peripheral vision, there is little or no enclosure.
32. *Articulation in building designs* considers the impact of building facades in stimulating the pedestrians and is categorized as highly articulated, somewhat articulated or with little or no articulation at all. Building articulation refers to the amount of architectural detail on the facade of a building. If the facade is a blank wall, it is considered unarticulated. On the other hand, if a building facade is embellished with architectural features and fenestrated with well-defined window openings, it may be considered articulated.
33. *Street orientation of buildings* considers the penetrability at ground floor level of buildings, and is categorized as streets having many windows, porches, entrances or moderate level of openings or long dead facades and boundary walls.
34. *Natural sights*, created through landscaping, is categorized as lots of greenery offering visual continuity, moderate level of greenery with intermittent placement or absolutely no natural attractions.

Annexure III: Proforma for Field Walkability Survey at Segment Level

A. GENERAL STREET ENVIRONMENT	
1. Segment type	
	Access street (dead-end/ continuous)
	Collector street
	Arterial/ sub-arterial road
2. Types of bldgs./ land uses (all that apply)	
	Mixed use
	Residential flatted
	Residential plotted
	Recreational (park/ playground)
	Office/ Commercial
	Institutional
	Workshops/ Garages/ Industrial
	Vacant/ undeveloped lot
3. Average building/ plot frontage	
	Narrow (less than 6.0 m) frontage
	Moderate (6.0 m to 9.0 m wide) frontage
	Wide (more than 9.0 m wide) frontage
4. Segment connectivity (no. of connections)	
	More than 6
	4 to 6
	Less than 4

B. PATH AVAILABILITY & QUALITY	
5. Type of pedestrian path (if none, skip B)	
	Pedestrian street closed to cars
	Sidewalk
	Footpath (worn dirt path)
6. Path location	
	More than 1.0 m from road kerb
	Within 1.0 m of road kerb
	Next to road kerb
7. Path width	
	More than 1.8 m
	From 1.2 m to 1.8 m
	Less than 1.2 m
8. Kerb type	
	Non-mountable
	Mountable
	No kerb
9. Path material	
	Precast pavers/ stone paving
	Concrete
	Brick paving
	Gravel/ dirt/ sand
10. Path condition (bumps/ potholes/ weeds)	
	Good (none of these)
	Moderate (some of these)
	Poor (many of these)
	Under repair
11. Path continuity	
	Mostly continuous
	Intermittent

Neighbourhood/ locality:	
Segment ID & length:	
Auditor ID:	
Date and time of survey:	

C. OBSTRUCTIONS TO WALKING	
12. Permanent obstructions (all that apply)	
	Poles, mesh of wires, etc
	Signage, public art, bus shelters
	Garbage bins/ heaps, benches, etc
	Trees, shrubs, bushes
	Open gutters, building projections, etc
13. Temporary obstructions (all that apply)	
	Street hawkers/ vendors
	Parked vehicles
	Portable signs/ furniture/ shop stands
	None
14. On street parking scenario	
	On street parking not allowed
	Moderate no. of vehicles (max.1/3 street façade)
	Parked vehicles dominate
15. Surface condition/ maintenance	
	Good (none of these)
	Moderate (some of these)
	Poor (many of these)
	Under repair

D. TRAFFIC SAFETY	
16. Traffic volume	
	Low to very low
	Medium
	High
17. Posted speed limit	
	Upto 30 kmph
	More than 30 kmph
	None posted
18. Number of traffic lanes to be crossed	
	1 to 2 lanes
	3 to 4 lanes
	5 or more lanes
19. Crossing aids (all that apply)	
	Zebra crossing
	Median refuge or traffic island
	Kerb extension
	Pedestrian signals
	None
20. Traffic calming devices (all that apply)	
	Traffic lights
	Stop signs/ bollards
	Traffic circle/ roundabout
	Speed bumps
	Chicanes/ chokers
	None

E. DISABILITY INFRASTRUCTURE
21. Any accessibility features (all that apply)
Kerb ramps
Tactile surfaces
Auditory signals
None

F. PEDESTRIAN AMENITIES
22. Availability of pedestrian amenities (all that apply)
Garbage bins
Street furniture
Drinking fountains
Public toilets
Bus stop/ shelter
Street vendors
23. Condition of pedestrian amenities
Properly working
Not maintained or in working state
24. Location of pedestrian amenities
Along pathway in the fixture/ planting zone
On pathway obstructing movement
25. Signage and public art
Provided and appropriately located
Provided but ill maintained/ at inappropriate location
Not provided at all
26. Overall cleanliness/ maintenance
Good
Fair
Poor
27. Street lighting
Pedestrian scale
Road oriented
None
28. Availability of shade (from trees/ buildings)
Continuous
Intermittent shade
No shade at all

G. SPATIAL QUALITY
29. Building setbacks from road edge
At edge
Upto 6 m
More than 6m
30. Building heights
1 to 2 storeyed
3 to 4 storeyed
More than 4 storeyed
31. Degree of enclosure (buildings/ trees)
Highly enclosed
Some enclosure
Little or no enclosure
32. Articulation in building designs
Highly articulated
Some articulation
Little or no articulation
33. Street orientation of buildings (penetrability at GF level)
Lot many windows/ porches/ entrances
Moderate level of openings
Long dead facades/ boundary walls
34. Natural sights (landscaping, views, etc)
Lot of greenery offering visual continuity
Moderate level of greenery, intermittent placement
Absolutely no natural attractions

H. SUBJECTIVE RATING (5-point Likert scale)
Very Bad 1; Bad 2; Avg. 3; Good 4; Very Good 5
35. General Street Environment
36. Pathway Availability and Quality
37. Obstructions to Walking
38. Traffic Safety
39. Disability Infrastructure
40. Pedestrian Amenities
41. Spatial Quality

Annexure IV: Questionnaire for Pedestrian Perception and Preference Survey

Name of the Neighbourhood/ Locality : _____

Socio-economic Profile

1. Gender

Male	Female

2. Age (in years)

0–15	15–30	30–50	>50

3. Monthly Household Income (in rupees)

< 10,000	10,000–50,000	50,000–2 lakhs	> 2 lakhs

4. Vehicle ownership

Bicycles	2-wheelers	Car/ jeep, etc.

Pedestrian Preference

5. How often do you prefer walking over driving?

Almost every time	Frequently	Sometimes	Very few times	Never

6. How do you rate the pedestrian facilities in your locality?

Very Good	Good	Average	Bad	Very Bad

7. If walkability conditions are enhanced, would you like to improve your walking habits?

Certainly	May think	Not at all	Don't know

8. What improvement would you like to have in pedestrian facilities?
   (Rank ALL as per your preference order)

Exclusive pathways for pedestrians
More shade along the pathway (from buildings/ trees)
Reduced and slow traffic on road
Clean litter free pathways
Remove obstacles and/or parking from footpaths
Improve surface conditions (remove potholes, etc.)
Provide/ improve amenities (benches, drinking fountains, etc.)
Easy access for the physically or visually disabled
Make the streets more attractive visually
Improved street lighting

Annexure V: Scores and Weights Assigned to the Parameters and Attributes of Walkability Survey

Codes			Weights assigned	Maximum scores
A	General street environment			15
A1	Segment type			3
		Access street	3	
		Collector street	2	
		Arterial/ sub-arterial road	1	
A2	Types of buildings/ land uses (all that apply)			6
		Residential flatted	1	
		Residential plotted	1	
		Mixed use	1	
		Recreational (park/playground)	1	
		Office/ commercial	1	
		Institutional	1	
		Workshops/ garages/ industrial	−1	
		Vacant/ undeveloped lot	−1	
A3	Average building/ plot frontage			3
		Narrow (less than 6.0 m) frontage	3	
		Moderate (6.0 m to 9.0 m wide) frontage	2	
		Wide (more than 9.0 m wide) frontage	1	
A4	Segment connectivity (number of connections)			3
		More than 6	3	
		4 to 6	2	
		Less than 4	1	
B	Pathway availability and quality			20
B5	Type of pedestrian path (if none, skip B)			3
		(if 1, skip B6) Pedestrian street closed to cars	3	
		Sidewalk	2	
		Footpath (worn dirt path)	1	
B6	Path location			3
		More than 1.0 m from road kerb	3	

	Within 1.0 m of road kerb	2	
	Next to road kerb	1	
B7	Path width		3
	More than 1.8 m	3	
	From 1.2 m to 1.8 m	2	
	Less than 1.2 m	1	
B8	Kerb type		3
	Mountable	3	
	Non-mountable	2	
	No kerb	1	
B9	Path material		3
	Precast pavers/ stone paving	3	
	Concrete/ brick paving	2	
	Gravel/ dirt/ sand	1	
B10	Path condition (bumps/ cracks/ potholes/ weeds)		3
	Good (none of these)	3	
	Moderate (some of these)	2	
	Poor (many of these) or under repair	1	
B11	Path continuity		2
	Mostly continuous	2	
	Intermittent	1	
C	**Obstructions to walking**		**6**
C12	Permanent obstructions (all that apply)		0
	Poles, mesh of wires, etc.	−1	
	Signage, public art, bus shelters	−1	
	Garbage bins/ heaps, benches, etc.	−1	
	Trees, shrubs, bushes	−1	
	Open gutters, building projections, etc.	−1	
C13	Temporary obstructions (all that apply)		0
	Street hawkers/ vendors	−1	
	Portable signs/ furniture/ shop stands	−1	
	Parked vehicles	−1	

C14	**On street parking scenario**		3
	On street parking not allowed	3	
	Moderate no. of parked vehicles (max.1/3 street façade)	2	
	Parked vehicles dominate	1	
C15	**Surface condition/ maintenance**		3
	Good (none of these)	3	
	Moderate (some of these)	2	
	Poor (many of these) or under repair	1	
D	**Traffic safety**		**18**
D16	**Traffic volume**		3
	Low to very low	3	
	Medium	2	
	High	1	
D17	**Posted speed limit**		3
	Up to 30 kmph	3	
	More than 30 kmph	2	
	None posted	1	
D18	**Number of traffic lanes to be crossed**		3
	1 to 2 lanes	3	
	3 to 4 lanes	2	
	5 or more lanes	1	
D19	**Crossing aids (all that apply)**		4
	Zebra crossing	1	
	Median refuge or traffic island	1	
	Kerb extension	1	
	Pedestrian signals	1	
D20	**Traffic calming devices (all that apply)**		5
	Traffic lights	1	
	Stop signs/ bollards	1	
	Traffic circle/ roundabout	1	
	Speed bumps	1	
	chicanes/ chokers	1	

E	**Disability infrastructure**		3
E21	Any accessibility features		
	Kerb ramps	1	
	Tactile surfaces	1	
	Auditory signals	1	
F	**Pedestrian amenities**		20
F22	Availability of pedestrian amenities (all that apply)		6
	Garbage bins	1	
	Street furniture	1	
	Drinking fountains	1	
	Public toilets	1	
	Bus stop/ shelter	1	
	Street vendors	1	
F23	Condition of pedestrian amenities		2
	Properly working	2	
	Not maintained or in working state	1	
F24	Location of pedestrian amenities		2
	Along the pathway in the fixture/ planting zone	2	
	On the pathway obstructing pedestrian movement	1	
F25	Signage and public art		2
	Provided and appropriately located	2	
	Provided but ill maintained and at inappropriate location	1	
	Not provided at all	0	
F26	Overall cleanliness/ maintenance (litter, rubbish, graffiti, etc.)		3
	Good	3	
	Fair	2	
	Poor	1	
F27	Street lighting		2
	Pedestrian scale	2	
	Road oriented	1	
	None	0	

F28	Availability of shade (from trees/ buildings)		3
	Continuous	3	
	Intermittent shade	2	
	No shade at all	1	
G	**Spatial quality**		**18**
G29	Building setbacks from sidewalk/ road edge		3
	At edge	3	
	Up to 6 m	2	
	More than 6m	1	
G30	Building heights		3
	More than 4 storeyed	3	
	3 to 4 storeyed	2	
	1 to 2 storeyed	1	
G31	Degree of enclosure (due to buildings/ trees)		3
	Highly enclosed	3	
	Some enclosure	2	
	Little or no enclosure	1	
G32	Articulation in building designs		3
	Highly articulated	3	
	Some articulation	2	
	Little or no articulation	1	
G33	Street orientation of buildings (penetrability at GF level)		3
	Lot many windows/ porches/ entrances	3	
	Moderate level of openings	2	
	Long dead facades/ boundary walls	1	
G34	Natural sights (landscaping, views, etc.)		3
	Lot of greenery offering visual continuity	3	
	Moderate level of greenery, intermittent placement	2	
	Absolutely no natural attractions	1	

H	Subjective rating (on a 5-point Likert scale) Very bad – 1; bad – 2; Average – 3; Good – 4; Very good – 5	10
A	General street environment	5
B	Pathway availability and quality	5
C	Obstructions to walking	5
D	Traffic safety	5
E	Disability infrastructure	5
F	Pedestrian amenities	5
G	Spatial quality	5

Index

A

Able-bodied pedestrian, 1
Accessibility to facilities, 22
At-grade pedestrian crossings, 55
Audit protocol, 80
Audit tools, 74
Auditory signal, 52
Average trip length, 66

B

Block length, 22, 24
Built environment, 16, 21
Bulb-outs, 37

C

Carriageway, 52,
Casual strolling trips, 2
Central financial assistance, 44
Central pollution control board, 4
Centre for science and environment, 59
Channelization islands, 37
Chicanes, 37
Chokers, 37
City development plans, 45
City fabric, 1, 2
Clarence A. Perry, 18, 19
Clarence Stein, 18
Clean air initiative for Asian cities, 56
Compact city, 11
Compound annual growth rate, 3
Comprehensive mobility plan for Amritsar, 66
Congress for the new urbanism, 11
Crossing aids, 77
Curb extensions, 37

D

Dead width, 49
Degree of enclosure, 78
Destination trips, 2
Disability infrastructure, 77, 132
Dispersed travel patterns, 5
Diverters, 38
Dynamic pedestrian behaviour, 2

E

Environmental planning collaborative, 58

F

Footpath surface, 49
Footpath width, 48
Freiburg, 24, 33
Frontage zone, 48
Furniture zone, 48

G

Green travel habits, 45
Groningen, 24
Guide blocks, 51
Guidelines for pedestrian facilities, 132

H

Home zones, 35, 38
Household interview surveys, 67

I

Indian penal code, 46
Indian roads congress, 42, 47
Institute for transportation and development policy, 58
Institute of urban transport, 43, 47

J

Jawaharlal Nehru Urban Renewable Mission, 45

K

Kerb extensions, 55
Kerb height, 49,
Kerb radius, 49
Kerb ramps, 50
Kerb type, 77

L

Land-use mix, 22, 25
Level of service, 49
Livable streets, 38
Liveability, 3, 9
Liveable communities, 12

M

Median islands, 37
Mid-block pedestrian crossings, 55
Ministry of urban development, 47
Mixed-land-use, 2
Modal split, 3
Motor vehicles act, 46
Mountable kerb, 50
Multi-functional zone, 53

N

N. L. Engelhardt, 18
National road safety and traffic management board bill, 47
National transport development policy committee, 46
National urban renewal mission, 44
National urban transport policy, 43
Neighbourhood environment walkability scale, 75
Neighbourhood unit, 18
Neighbourhood walkability, 72
Neo-traditional development, 13
New pedestrianism, 12, 14
New urbanism, 11
Non-motorized transport, 68

O

On-street parking scenario, 77

P

Para-transit, 46
Path condition, 77
Path continuity, 77
Path location, 77
Path material, 77
Path width, 77
Pedestrian amenities, 78, 132
Pedestrian crossings, 54
Pedestrian design toolkit, 57
Pedestrian environment data scan, 65, 75
Pedestrian environment review system, 75
Pedestrian facilities, 7
Pedestrian opinion surveys, 67
Pedestrian perception, 79
Pedestrian preferences, 80
Pedestrian scale lighting, 54
Pedestrian sensitivity, 1
Pedestrian village, 14
People-centric, 131
Permanent obstructions, 77
Permeability, 23
Planning module, 18
Population density, 22
Private transport mode, 3
Public art, 30
Public transport, 6, 46

R

Raised crosswalks, 37
Refuge island, 55
Residential density, 73
Residents' feedback, 73
Right-of-way, 48, 58

Road infrastructure, 3
Road network inventory, 67
Rumble strips, 36

S

Safety bollards, 55
Shared zones, 34, 35
Shared-use paths, 35
Sidewalks, 22, 29
Signage, 22, 30
Social acceptability, 6
Spatial quality, 78
Specific area plans, 44
Speed bumps, 36
Speed humps, 36
Speed tables, 37
Static pedestrian activity, 2
Street closures, 38
Street connectivity, 16
Street crossings, 22, 29
Street furniture, 46, 52
Street geometry, 22, 29
Street hierarchy, 77
Street lighting, 22, 30
Street network, 22, 24
Street trees, 22, 28
Street vending, 58
Street-oriented buildings, 22, 25
Surface condition, 77
Surface materials, 22, 30

T

Tabletop crossings, 55
Tactile paving, 51
Temporary obstructions, 77
Thermal comfort, 132

Traditional neighbourhood development, 12, 13
Traditional urbanism, 12
Traffic calming elements, 55
Traffic circles, 37
Traffic volume, 77
Traffic-reduction engineering techniques, 35
Transit-oriented development, 12
Trip lengths, 7, 67

U

Urban realm, 16

V

Vauban, 24
Vehicle-centric, 131
Vehicular emission, 5
Verkehrsberuhigung, 36
Visual enclosure, 22, 26

W

Walk trips, 66
Walkability assessment, 73
Walkability index, 67
Walking audit, 74
Walking surface, 49
Warning blocks, 51
Woonerf, 35, 38